Praise for
The Mystery of Incomprehensible Love

"The spiritual message of Catherine Mectilde de Bar is very beautiful and deep, and deserves to be better known. The texts gathered in this volume help us to understand how the humble and silent presence of Jesus in the Eucharist is a priceless gift for the Church. We find in this mystery of love everything we need for our Christian life." — FR. JACQUES PHILIPPE, author of *Searching for and Maintaining Peace*

"When I first discovered Mother Mectilde at the age of 18, my soul rejoiced and I knew that I had to go to a monastery where her teaching was practiced. Her writings bring me ever deeper into the Mystery of God's infinite Love; they help me enter into the *Mysterium Fidei* of Holy Mass. She made me a daughter of the Most Blessed Sacrament and a daughter, too, of Our Lady. You who hold this book in your hands, you will find real life in it. Don't just read it, *live* it." — MOTHER IMMACULATA FRANKEN, OSBap, Prioress of the Benedictines of Perpetual Adoration, Tegelen, The Netherlands

"We learn from the best, which is why we look to the saints to help us. We are only beginners, but they are the experts, the 'olympic champions' of the spiritual life: St. Faustina and the Divine Mercy, St Teresa of Avila and contemplative prayer, St. Therese of Lisieux and her 'Little Way' of trust and surrender, and now Mother Mectilde and Eucharistic love. Although she lived more than 300 years ago, her words are not archaic but vibrant: she articulates to perfection what it looks like to live a Eucharistic life today. She speaks like a woman in love, and her words can ignite a fire in your soul. When I go to daily adoration, this little gem of a book will be my *vademecum* for quite a while!" — SR. JULIA MARY DARRENKAMP, Fsp

"Mother Mectilde's spiritual message unveils a loving solidarity with Christ and an invitation to enter into His saving mission. It is a message both encouraging and challenging. Immersing us in the mysteries of Jesus, she advocates a deep surrender of faith in response to His gift of Himself. She recommends silent adoration of the Eucharist, devout participation at Mass, and vital concern for the salvation of others, especially those who are indifferent. A daughter of St. Benedict, her vision is filled with ecclesial, liturgical, sacramental, and profoundly mystical insight." — DR. ANTHONY LILLES, author of *Fire from Above: Christian Contemplation and Mystical Wisdom*

"This book constitutes a great blessing for the English-speaking world. It introduces Mother Mectilde de Bar, a truly remarkable figure from the seventeenth century (the *siècle d'or* of French spirituality), who up to now has barely been known outside of the monastic tradition she founded: the Benedictine Nuns of Perpetual Adoration, now happily augmented by the monks of Silverstream Priory in Ireland. In reading the excerpts chosen for the anthology, I found myself reminded not only of many insights in the Sacred Scriptures and the Rule of Saint Benedict, but also of the writings of Saints Elizabeth of the Trinity, Thérèse of Lisieux, Louis-Marie de Montfort, Peter Julian Eymard, and Blessed Concepción Cabrera de Armida, to name only a few. These passages harmonize with so many of theirs, even while she retains her own unique insights and tonality. She emphasizes adoration, reparation, and victimhood in ways that transcend the centuries and relate also to the messages of Fatima and Saint Faustina. My profound gratitude to those who have brought this wonderful publication to the light of day." — MSGR. ARTHUR B. CALKINS, author of *Totus Tuus: Pope Saint John Paul II's Program of Marian Consecration and Entrustment*

"The French School of spirituality shaped the minds and hearts of saints and servants of God in France during the seventeenth century. The life of Mère Mectilde du Saint Sacrement spanned most of that 'great century': she was born during the lifetime of Bérulle, the School's founding father, and died when St Louis-Marie de Montfort, the last of the great Bérullians, was a seminarian. Her spiritual doctrine is equally comprehensive in the School's major themes: the states of the Word incarnate (Bérulle), the Hearts of Jesus and Mary (St John Eudes), Our Lady as our principal example and helper in assisting at the Holy Sacrifice of the Mass and receiving Holy Communion (St Louis-Marie). But Mère Mectilde orders these tremendous insights according to Benedictine and liturgical principles, and expresses them with attractive simplicity. This anthology, in its wonderfully lucid translation, should be in the hands of every priest and religious, especially Benedictines, in the English-speaking world. It is indeed a book for every Christian who desires to be a saint." — FR. JOHN SAWARD, author of *Cradle of Redeeming Love: The Theology of the Christmas Mystery*

The
Mystery of
Incomprehensible
Love

The Mystery of Incomprehensible Love

The Eucharistic Message of Mother Mectilde of the Blessed Sacrament

Foreword by
Dom Mark Kirby, OSB

Angelico Press

First published in the
USA and UK by Angelico Press
© Angelico Press 2020
Originally published in French as
Le message eucharistique de mère
Mectilde du Saint Sacrement 1614–1698
edited by Joseph Daoust (Paris: Téqui, 1981)
© Éditions Pierre Téqui, 8 rue de Mézières, 75006 Paris

For information, address:
Angelico Press
169 Monitor St.
Brooklyn, NY 11222
angelicopress.com

ISBN 978-1-62138-521-9 (pbk)
ISBN 978-1-62138-522-6 (cloth)
ISBN 978-1-62138-526-4 (ebook)

Cover Design: Michael Schrauzer

CONTENTS

Foreword

THIS ANTHOLOGY of the writings of Catherine de Bar (1614–1698)—in religion, Mother Mectilde of the Blessed Sacrament—is a timely introduction to the doctrine of a great teacher of the interior life. Mectilde of the Blessed Sacrament shines brightly, not only among the constellation of seventeenth-century France's luminous masters of the interior life, but also among the Church's surest guides to holiness. Mother Mectilde is, according to Dom Jean Leclercq, "stupendously Benedictine."[1] By this, the learned monk meant, I think, that one readily finds in Mother Mectilde the essential characteristics of Benedictine holiness as given in Chapter 58 of the Holy Rule: a true seeking of God marked by zeal for the Divine Office and eagerness for obedience and humiliations.

Mother Mectilde's English-speaking spiritual progeny, now made up of monks, nuns, and oblates in England, Ireland, the Netherlands, the United States, and Uganda, have long expressed the desire for an accessible, familiar contact with the vast corpus of her writings. The present volume presents a discourse on the Solemnity of Thursday followed by short passages on the Holy Mass, the practice of frequent Communion, dispositions required for Communion, the spirit of adoration and worship, the virtues we draw from the Holy Eucharist, and the way in which participating in Our Lord's mysteries conforms us to Him and His dispositions. It is my hope and expectation that all who read these texts will find sparks capable of enkindling the fire of prayer in the heart.

---

[1] See the Afterword.

1

The message of Mother Mectilde of the Blessed Sacrament is by no means limited to those who, hidden in a Benedictine cloister, follow more closely in her footsteps. Her message continues to bring counsel, wisdom, and comfort to men and women of every state of life who have discovered that the call to holiness is universal, and that holiness can, in some way, be summed up in the three words that express the particular grace of Mother Mectilde's life: adoration, abandonment, and adherence.

Adoration opens the soul to grace. It is a sinking into nothingness in the presence of God who is all. Mother Mectilde frequently uses the French word *anéantissement*. In this anthology the word has been translated as *ennothingment*. In one of her letters, Mother Mectilde writes: "You must make your way towards ennothingment. Otherwise, you will always be unhappy." Ennothingment is the ground of adoration. It situates a man rightly before God, in what Gerard Manley Hopkins describes as being "lost, all lost in wonder."

> Godhead here in hiding, whom I do adore,
> Masked by these bare shadows, shape and nothing more,
> See, Lord, at thy service low lies here a heart
> Lost, all lost in wonder at the God thou art.[2]

Abandonment is the spontaneous expression of a childlike confidence in God. Abandonment occurs on nearly every page of Mother Mectilde's correspondence. She understands and lives abandonment as the only response possible to the revelation of the fatherhood of God.

Adherence is another way of expressing what the English biblical lexicon sometimes calls "cleaving," in the sense of being intimately united or joined unto another. Mother Mectilde's adherence to God in Christ is an unconditional obedience to all that God wills or permits. It is also the union of the branch with the

---

[2] From the poet's translation of the "Adoro te devote" by St. Thomas Aquinas.

vine, of the member of the body with its head, and of the bride with her Bridegroom.

The God-seeking journey of Mother Mectilde of the Blessed Sacrament, though rigorously consistent throughout her long life, was marked by danger, exile, illness, poverty, and uncertainties on all sides. If Catherine Mectilde de Bar is, as I believe, a woman of the stature of a Gertrude the Great, a Teresa of Avila, and a Marie of the Incarnation (Guyart-Martin), her message must have about it a certain timeless and universal quality: a resonance in the life of the Church in every age. Mother Mectilde's life and mission are a vivid and compelling demonstration of the role of cloistered women in the Church today and in every age. Her writings, steeped in Sacred Scripture and in the liturgical tradition that formed her as a Benedictine nun, reveal a woman of profound human insights and of supernatural wisdom.

Mother Mectilde presents the grace of Baptism as ordered to a mystical participation in the victimhood of Christ by reception of the adorable mysteries of His Body and Blood in Holy Communion. In affirming this, she elucidates with the brightness of her own experience the *Eucharistic form of the Christian life* that Pope Benedict XVI set forth in *Sacramentum Caritatis*:

> Here the Eucharistic celebration appears in all its power as the source and summit of the Church's life, since it expresses at once both the origin and the fulfilment of the new and definitive worship of God, the *logike latreia*. Saint Paul's exhortation to the Romans in this regard is a concise description of how the Eucharist makes our whole life a spiritual worship pleasing to God: "I appeal to you therefore, my brothers, by the mercies of God, to present your bodies as a living sacrifice, holy and acceptable to God, which is your spiritual worship" (Rom 12:1). In these words the new worship appears as a total self-offering made in communion with the whole Church. The Apostle's insistence on the offering of our bodies emphasizes the

concrete human reality of a worship which is anything but disincarnate. The Bishop of Hippo goes on to say that "this is the sacrifice of Christians: that we, though many, are one body in Christ. The Church celebrates this mystery in the sacrament of the altar, as the faithful know, and there she shows them clearly that in what is offered, she herself is offered." Catholic doctrine, in fact, affirms that the Eucharist, as the sacrifice of Christ, is also the sacrifice of the Church, and thus of all the faithful. This insistence on sacrifice—a "making sacred"—expresses all the existential depth implied in the transformation of our human reality as taken up by Christ (cf. Phil 3:12).[3]

The vocational journey of Catherine Mectilde de Bar was marked by unforeseen turns, by sufferings of body and soul, by new beginnings, by constant displacements, and by an immutable stability in the One Thing Necessary (cf. Lk 10:42). In this, Mother Mectilde speaks to the young men and women of today who must follow their vocations with an immense courage in the midst of uncertainty, movement, and rapid change. In a time when many shrink back from saying a "Yes" that binds until death, Mother Mectilde shows that happiness lies, not in the subjective indulgence of endless and tortuous discernments, but in the simplicity of a decision made in faith and in abandonment to Divine Providence.

The past fifty years have witnessed a weakening of faith in the Real Presence of Christ in the Most Holy Eucharist and of faith in the Holy Mass as a real though unbloody sacrifice making present the mystery of Christ, Priest and Victim, in His oblation to the Father. Mother Mectilde's lucid and fiery Eucharistic doctrine defies every attempt to empty the Mass of its essentially sacrificial character as irreformably defined by the Council of Trent. The study of the life and writings of Catherine Mectilde

---

[3] Post-Synodal Apostolic Exhortation *Sacramentum Caritatis*, §70.

de Bar constitute a precious *locus theologicus* in which it becomes possible to engage certain key teachings of the Council of Trent with the authentic magisterium of subsequent critical periods in such a way as to arrive at a fruitful synthesis of liturgical continuity, Eucharistic theology, and mystical experience. Mother Mectilde's commitment to perpetual adoration of the Most Blessed Sacrament corresponds to a contemporary yearning, especially among young people, for a personal, transforming encounter with the Face of God. Her intimate and cordial relationship with the Blessed Virgin Mary is a model of life-giving Marian piety.

Mother Mectilde's attachment to the sacred liturgy, to the worthy celebration of the Holy Mysteries in an environment marked by beauty, by profound reverence, and by a humble decorum, is an invitation to recover what shaped and expressed the faith of past generations while, at the same time, recognizing every effort at growth and progress duly undertaken in organic continuity, without rupture and, above all, in charity.

> In the history of the liturgy there is growth and progress, but no rupture. What earlier generations held as sacred, remains sacred and great for us too, and it cannot be all of a sudden entirely forbidden or even considered harmful. It behooves all of us to preserve the riches which have developed in the Church's faith and prayer, and to give them their proper place.[4]

Catherine Mectilde de Bar lived in a time marked by superstition, sorcery, dalliance with the powers of darkness, blasphemy, and sacrilege. Distressing events in churches on every continent have demonstrated that global society today has more in common with war-torn 17th-century France than one might think. Mother Mectilde bound herself in self-sacrificing love to the perpetrators of such horrible crimes, offering herself as a victim of

---

[4] Pope Benedict XVI, Letter to the Bishops on the Occasion of the Apostolic Letter *Summorum Pontificum*, 7 July 2007.

reparation, that is, as a sacrifice irrevocably made over to God. In so doing, she sought to supply for the love and adoration denied God by those who hate Him and outrage His holiness while, at the same time, praying God to show them mercy and grace them with repentance.

Finally, Catherine Mectilde de Bar is an icon of the kind of spiritual motherhood needed in the Church today, not only in monastic and religious communities, but in every context where the Church is being born, and born again, of the Most Holy Eucharist. *Ecclesia de Eucharistia*. Mother Mectilde demonstrates that the altar itself—the place set apart for the immolation of the Divine Victim—becomes a wellspring of supernatural fecundity in the life of every soul who, adhering to the Holy Sacrifice, enters into the victimhood of Christ and, with Him, adores the Father in the Holy Spirit.

The Mystery of Incomprehensible Love seeks to introduce Mother Mectilde of the Blessed Sacrament to an English-speaking readership. Those who read her words, while tarrying in her company, will be drawn ineluctably to seek out the hiddenness of the Host. In this one thing Mother Mectilde's words will have fulfilled that for which she wrote them: "I sat down under his shadow, whom I desired: and his fruit was sweet to my palate" (Cant 2:3).

Dom Mark Kirby, OSB
Silverstream Priory
Feast of St. Scholastica
February 10, 2020

A Note on Sources

The biography of Mother Mectilde by Canon G. A. Simon was originally published as "Mechtilde du Saint-Sacrement et son temps (1614–1698)," in *Priez sans cesse. Trois cents ans de prière: Melanges a l'occasion du tricentaire de L'Institute des Benedictines de l'adoration perpetuelle du Saint Sacrement* (Paris: Desclée de Brouwer, 1953), and translated by a Benedictine oblate.

"On the Solemnity of Thursday" was translated by a Benedictine monk from *La journée religieuse les Bénédictines du Très-Saint Sacrement, suivie des exercises spirituels par la V. Mère Mectilde du Saint-Sacrement, Institutrice de l'Adoration perpétuelle*, 3rd edition (Lille: L. Lefort, 1859), 230–45.

The remaining texts were translated by a Benedictine oblate from *Le message eucharistique de mère Mectilde du Saint Sacrement 1614–1698*, edited by Joseph Daoust (Paris: Tequi, 1981), 59–156. The numbers listed after each quotation refer to the central index of the writings of Mother Mectilde prepared by the nuns of the Benedictines of Perpetual Adoration, which, due to the quantity of material, has been in progress for some decades.

The essay by Dom Jean Leclercq was translated by a Benedictine monk from *Non date tregua a Dio: Lettere alle monache 1641–1697* (Milan: Jaca Book, 1979), 11–24, with reference to the French original: "Une école de spiritualité bénédictine datant du XVIIe siècle: Les Bénédictines de l'Adoration Perpétuelle," *Studia Monastica* 18.2 (1976): 433–52.

Selections
from the Writings of
Mother Mectilde

On the Solemnity of Thursday

Introduction by a Benedictine Monk

C ATHERINE-MECTILDE DE BAR is, without any doubt, the most Eucharistic soul in what was a Eucharistic century *par excellence*, a century of saints surpassing all others, *le grand siècle*, the great century of France's mystic invasion, and the full flowering of the Council of Trent's renewal of the Church in holiness. In this splendid text, Mother Mectilde de Bar pours out her soul in a torrent of amazement and thanksgiving and adoration. She sets forth why, in her particular Benedictine observance, Thursday is celebrated as a weekly return to the Cenacle where Our Lord instituted the Sacrament of His Love, and as a weekly festival of Corpus Christi.

But why does Mother Mectilde say that Thursday is a day of *Pascha*? How are we to understand this affirmation, which, at first, seems surprising to those who think more in chronological than in theological terms? Mother Mectilde's affirmation is rooted in a profoundly intuitive experience of the liturgy of Holy Thursday, whose Introit is a synthesis of the entire Paschal Mystery:

> It is right for us to glory in the Cross of our Lord Jesus Christ, in whom is our salvation, life, and resurrection: through whom we have been saved and set free. (cf. Gal 6:14)

The Church's liturgy does not wait until Easter Sunday to sing of "salvation, life, and resurrection." It is the Paschal Triduum in its entirety, beginning with the evening Mass *In Coena Domini* on

11

Thursday, that actualizes the mysteries of Our Lord's Passion, death, and resurrection. Holy Thursday includes Good Friday, Holy Saturday, and Easter Sunday, and these days include within themselves the mystery already announced, realized, and communicated in the Cenacle on Thursday in the Most Holy Sacrament of the Altar. To appreciate Mother Mectilde's intuition, we must think with an inclusive "both/and" rather than an exclusive "either/or." It is not a question of Thursday *or* Sunday, but of Thursday *and* Sunday: Thursday contains, as in a kernel, the complete mystery that unfolds over Friday and Saturday, to emerge into a glorious light on Sunday. Mother Mectilde's affirmation springs from her own contemplative participation in the liturgy of the Church, and from her intuitive grasp that the liturgy is played out in *kairos*—God's moment, the liturgical *hodie*—rather than in *chronos*, the human way of measuring time.

Mother Mectilde focused on Thursday, and established it in her Institute as a kind of weekly *Fête-Dieu*,[1] because she understood that the Most Holy Eucharist is the sacramental demonstration of the Cross. Is this not what the Apostle teaches? "For as often as you shall eat this bread, and drink the chalice, you shall show forth the death of the Lord, until he comes" (1 Cor 11:26).

The Most Holy Eucharist makes present the Cross as the altar of Christ, Eternal High Priest and spotless Victim. The Most Holy Sacrament of the Altar is the sacrifice of the Cross set before the eyes of faith, not as something dim and ineffectual, but as an astonishing inbreaking, here and now, of "the power of God and the wisdom of God"(1 Cor 1:24). This is, to borrow the expression of John Paul II, the source of Mother Mectilde's "Eucharistic amazement." This is the realization that leaves us, together with her and with the saints of every age, as Gerard Manley Hopkins put it, "lost, all lost in wonder."

---

[1] The French way of referring to the feast of Corpus Christi.

A further comment is in order before reading the text. In the second paragraph, Mother Mectilde speaks of "the victims of the Holy Sacrament," referring to herself and her fellow Benedictines of perpetual adoration. The word *victim* frightens some people; it exercises an unhealthy attraction over others; and for still others has an unpleasantly melodramatic ring about it. When Mother Mectilde de Bar uses the word *victim*, what exactly does she mean?

First of all, she uses it as the proper title of those who are vowed to adoration of the Most Holy Sacrament under the Rule of Saint Benedict in her Institute. While others, she says, may enter religious life to save their own souls and gain eternal glory in heaven, the Benedictine of the Most Holy Sacrament must so forget herself, and even the needs of her own soul, that she sacrifices all self-interest and enters the monastery for one reason only: to adore and glorify the Most Holy Sacrament of the Altar, and to make up, by her sacrifice of all spiritual self-interest, for those who never adore Our Lord in the Sacrament of His Love or, even worse, offend Him by unspeakable sins of irreverence and sacrilege.

Secondly, she uses the word *victim* in the same way the texts of the sacred liturgy use it. One could cite here any number of Secrets and Postcommunions from both the Temporal and Sanctoral Masses. A victim is a living being made over to God alone in so radical and irrevocable a way that she no longer has any life outside of life in God, for God, and by God. The liturgical use of the term *victim* makes it very clear that this is the ordinary state of anyone who receives Holy Communion consciously and devoutly. By being atoned (at-oned, joined) to the Divine Victim, the Lamb of God, one becomes a single *victim* with Him, that is, an offering made over to the Father in a holocaust of love.

Thirdly, she uses the word to express the profound communion of the soul with Our Lord in the Sacrament of His Love, where He is forever the *Christus passus*, Christ in the very act of

His immolation and self-offering to the Father. Our Lord present in the tabernacle is not there in a state of suspended animation or divine inertia; He is present in the Most Blessed Sacrament as He is in the sanctuary of Heaven: the pure victim, the holy victim, the spotless victim, offered at every moment to the Father, in the Holy Spirit. One who adores the Blessed Sacrament will be, sooner or later, drawn into a mystic participation in the victimhood of the Lamb.

The Text of Mother Mectilde

THURSDAY: one can name it the day of the magnificences and profusions of divine love. It is on this day that Jesus Christ unfurls all the grandeurs of His munificence and gives to men the most incomprehensible proof of His charity, by instituting the Most Holy Sacrament of the Eucharist. O precious day! Day that we shall never know how to celebrate enough! Holy day, happy day, of which every instant must be infinitely precious to us who have the honor of being wholly consecrated to this august mystery.

For the victims of the Holy Sacrament, Thursday must be a day of Pascha, a day of solemnity and of rejoicing. This day is so abundant in graces that one can say that it exhausts all that Our Lord Jesus Christ is and can do. What more can He do after the institution of the divine Eucharist? What is there that is not [contained] in this august mystery?

Sunday is held in singular veneration among all Christians, because it is dedicated and consecrated in a special manner to the Most Holy Trinity. One author has said that so abundant in blessings is this day that all creatures participate in them, each according to its nature and capacity. If this is so of Sunday, what then must be said of Thursday? The same God whom we adore on Sunday in Himself, gives Himself entirely to us on Thursday. Thursday is the day of God's great communications to His creatures. Oh! who is not ravished by the infinite goodness of the King of kings! He gives us all that He has, all that He is, *all*—without reservation.

Jesus, says Saint John, *having loved His own, loved them to the end*.[2] And, in effect, what greater mark of love could He give them than to institute the Holy Eucharist? How great is the marvel that He works for us on this day, and who shall be able to understand it? It is here that all must remain in the silence of admiration. A God makes Himself our food! O astonishing prodigy! What are all the miracles worked by Jesus Christ during the course of His earthly life in comparison to this one? What a spectacle! What bounty! What charity! A God who gives Himself to us! O love! He who with three fingers sustains the universe is held by the priest. He who commands all of nature obeys a being who is nothing. He who is all-powerful makes Himself so dependent that He is in the power of His creatures; they carry Him, they bring Him wherever they choose. This is too much. Your charity, my Savior, goes even to excess! O incomprehensible miracle! Mystery forever inconceivable! No, the thought of man would not know how to attain it.

Man cannot understand; but man can love, man can adore. We, especially, who by a special favor see the Most Holy Sacrament exposed on our altars every Thursday[3]—with what fervor should we not be animated? The solemnity of Thursday must be for us a solemnity forever new; it must also set our hearts ablaze with a love that is new. Let us not settle for drawing people to

---

[2] Cf. Jn 13:1.

[3] Eucharistic *adoration* must not be confused with Eucharistic *exposition*. Among the Benedictines of the Most Holy Sacrament, exposition of the Blessed Sacrament was limited to Thursdays and to the following feasts: Christmas, Circumcision, Epiphany, Easter, Pentecost, Annunciation, Assumption, Saint Benedict on March 21 and July 11, and Saint Scholastica. On all the other days, the perpetual adoration was carried out before the closed tabernacle.

the feet of Jesus the Host by the outward worship that we render Him more particularly on this day. Let us redouble our readiness to attend to His holy presence. Let the whole Community, if possible, remain in adoration to recognize the gift that the Eternal Father has made to the world in Jesus Christ, His Son, in this God whose love constrains Him to stay among men even unto the consummation of the ages.

In the Eucharist, our adorable Savior has a love that surpasses all other loves; His heart is open to all as a wellspring abounding in graces and in mercies. How hard one would have to be not to be touched by so excessive a kindness, not to be burned by this most ardent charity! How obliged we are to Jesus Christ for having readily willed to set, in this way, Paradise on earth! A God makes Himself captive for us! He is in our new arks like a prisoner in his jail cell! How happy we are to possess in this way our most lovable Savior in the Most Holy Sacrament, since we have in this august mystery the One whom the angels and the saints love and adore in heaven, the One who is the object of their eternal beatitude. What marvels! Can one contemplate them without falling into an eternal ravishment? Oh! the prodigious invention of divine charity! What is it, my God, what is the creature that You fill it so with the abundance of your graces? Man is but a nothing, and you are not satisfied with having created him, redeemed him, shed even the last drop of your blood for him, dying for his salvation. You yourself still give yourself to him... O ineffable grace! O inestimable gift!

If we but had a little faith, what meditations, what sublime contemplations would the sight of a God giving Himself to man not inspire in us! But no, we are blind and know not how to appreciate so great a happiness; we are insensible and Jesus the Host does not touch us; we are so miserable that the least trifle occupies us entirely, and we remain closed to heaven's most precious graces, to the infinite benefits of our God. Have we ever duly given thanks for the ineffable gift of the Eucharist? What

thanksgivings have we made for it? Alas!, one must say in groan-
ing that the greater number of men never even think of Jesus
present among them.

A God—greatness, power, richness itself—reduces Himself
to nothing for us in the Host, and we think no more of it than
one would of something commonplace and ordinary. O stupid-
ity! Oh, the ingratitude of men! One does not think of Jesus
Christ in the Eucharist and, yet, is this not, of all mysteries, the
most divine, of all marvels the most prodigious, the most inconceivable? What has one said of this divine mystery up until the
present that in any way approaches the reality of it? What are the
most learned men's discourses next to what it is in truth? No,
no, there is not a tongue that would know how to express the
grandeurs, the riches hidden in our tabernacles. It is an abyss
impenetrable to the human spirit. You Yourself, O God, reveal to
some privileged soul the secret of this mystery, and put your
spirit within her, that she might speak of it worthily, for, in
truth, we know nothing of it.

No, no, we do not know what the Eucharist is. We believe in
this mystery, but it is with a faith that is languishing and unre-
fined; we are content to believe in the presence of Jesus Christ
on the altar, without deepening anything, without penetrating
ourselves through with the wonders that He works there. What
is this, then, O my God, what is this great Sacrament, so incomprehensible, so admirable, so miraculous? What is Jesus the
Host, and what does He do when He descends into His creature,
when He loses Himself in her by Holy Communion? O my soul,
if thou but knew the gift of God! *Si scires donum Dei!*[4] If thou but
understood something of this mystery of faith, *mysterium fidei*! If
thou but knew the One who hides Himself, who buries Himself,
who annihilates Himself in thee? If thou couldst but plumb the
depths of His love! Wouldst thou be able to live a single instant

---

[4] Cf. Jn 4:10.

without giving thyself to Him? A God who visits us, a God who gives Himself to us; He comes to raise us up from our woes and to deliver us from the tyranny of sin—and we do not die of love for Him? Ah, I pray You, lift the veil that conceals You from our eyes; let the torch of faith illumine us, that we might fathom all that You are, all that You do for us on the altar and in our hearts!

Let us try to recognize the excess of divine charity, and let this be the measure of our gratitude and of our love. What shall we give to God to pay Him for giving Himself to us? Let us not search outside of ourselves; it is ourselves that He asks for, it is our love that He purchases with His own. He gives Himself to us only so that we might give ourselves to Him. He asks for ourselves, not that we should be *His* happiness, but that He should be *ours*; because the felicity of the creature is found only in the possession of God. Oh! Far too greedy is the soul for whom Jesus Christ is not enough! All of us, let us find our contentment in Him and leave to Him all the rest! He wants to be our unique possession, to the exclusion of ourselves and of all that is created. My God, what more can we desire after having received You in our hearts? In giving Yourself to us, do You not give all things with Yourself? No, no, the Holy Sacrament alone is enough for a true victim; she finds all in Him; she has no need of anything else to sanctify herself, to perfect herself; for her, all is contained in the sacred Eucharistic Bread. Jesus Christ sacrificed is all her science, all her love, all her treasure. She finds in Him the lights and the knowledge she needs.

Let us draw near to Him and we shall be enlightened! *Accedite ad eum et illuminamini.*[5] Jesus Christ, silent in the Host, carries out, as He did during His mortal life, the office of Master and of Doctor. A saint said that the Cross was, as it were, a pulpit for this Man-God. One can say the same thing of our tabernacles: the different states that He there assumes are so many lessons

[5] Ps 33:6 [34:5]. Come ye to him and be enlightened.

that He is giving us: He wants us to live by His Eucharistic life, His life sacrificed, His life annihilated, His life of absolute death to all created things. Let us deepen this divine mystery; we shall see that the Author of Life is there in a state of death, that the Wisdom of the Father remains in silence, that Infinite Being encloses Himself in an imperceptible particle, that the Sovereign and All-Powerful obeys a weak mortal.

Truly, it is in the Holy Eucharist that Jesus Christ is, according to the language of Scripture, *the hidden God, the self-emptied God* ...[6] And what reduces Him to this profound exinanition? Why, little satisfied with having become a mortal man capable of suffering, does He make Himself, in this way, His creature's most ordinary food? Always the same answer: *Jesus Christ has loved us.* When will it be given us to render love for love? Let us love, O my sisters, let us love without delay this lovable Savior who hides the brightness of His glory so that we might have a way to draw near to Him, who empties Himself of His grandeurs to honor His Father in our place, who ceaselessly sacrifices Himself to deflect from our heads the rigors of divine justice. Let us employ all our care to adore Him well; let us place all our glory in rendering Him the homage we owe Him. Let us really be victims, according to the commitment we have made. Are we not very happy that God has chosen us to belong to Him in so particular a manner, and to keep Him company in His sacred mystery? For whom does He put Himself more specially in the Host, if not for us? One can say that Jesus Christ Himself produced us at the altar for Himself; because the work He accomplished in establishing this Institute immolates us and sacrifices us altogether to His self-emptied greatness in the adorable Eucharist. Let us deepen the holiness of this work and, seized with astonishment at the sight of our unworthiness, we shall cry out in transport: "O God, is it possible that you willed to suffer such poor and

---

[6] Cf. Is 45:15; Phil 2:7.

wretched creatures in Your temple and in the place of Your perpetual adorations?" Let us cast ourselves low, let us empty ourselves out, in considering God's bounties for us. O my Savior! Let Your sanctity purify us! Let it render us worthy of adoring eternally Your divine Sacrament! Let us live henceforth only to glorify You, as so many hosts consecrated to Your august Majesty, and who, consequently, have no right at all over themselves!

By the vow of victimhood, in no way do we belong any more to ourselves; Jesus Christ claims all His rights over us. Our life, our movements, our thoughts, our operations both inward and outward, all belongs to Him; we are, in a word, daughters of the Holy Sacrament. How august and mysterious this name is! We are daughters of the Holy Sacrament—that is to say, we must be altogether entered into and passed over into Jesus Christ, with crosses for our inheritance with Him, with disgraces, humiliations, rejections, contradictions, sufferings, temptations, and whatsoever crucifies our nature. There is all our portion, there our inheritance. We would be mistaken to expect anything else; we cannot be victims without the sword, without the cord, without torment, without sorrow, without death.

Associated to Jesus Christ in His quality of pledge for sinners, let us ever have before our eyes the obligations that this title confers and let us not forget that we are victims of the divine justice. By our [religious] profession, we only began our sacrifice; it must be consummated and brought to its final perfection. For that, crosses are needed, agonies, and annihilations. Let us, then, run towards all that crucifies our nature. This is the example given us by Jesus Christ. This is what He expects of us. This is what we engaged ourselves to do in entering the Institute. Without crosses we would not truly be daughters of the Holy Sacrament; without crosses, Jesus Christ would not be able to take His delights in us. He gave Himself and still gives Himself to us entirely. He wills that, in the same way, we should give ourselves entirely to Him to become victim-hosts of His justice.

By the sacrifice of ourselves, we shall yet arrive at establishing the life of Jesus Christ in us. This is His desire: He wills that we should live for Him as He lives for His Father, and so be able, all of us, to say with the Apostle: *I live, no longer I, but it is Jesus Christ who lives in me.*[7] In this way, God will be uniquely and sovereignly glorified in us, for time and for eternity. Live no longer, then, except for our Victim; let us convert ourselves totally in Him; He expects this of our fidelity, and we owe it to our precious title of daughters of the Holy Sacrament. Let us work at renouncing ourselves, at mortification and, as Saint Paul says, *let us accomplish in us what is lacking to the Passion of Jesus Christ.*[8]

To strengthen our weakness, have recourse to Our Lord. Let us raise up our courage and our confidence. Jesus Christ suffers and dies *for us*; let us draw our strength from His weakness, and our life from His death. Pray Him to come into us, to show that He is our God and our absolute Sovereign. In spite of all the opposition and the repugnances of our nature, let Him bring us entirely into subjection to His empire, to His power, and to His laws. Let us make to Him as perfect a sacrifice of ourselves as He desires.

When we are before the Most Holy Sacrament, we must not be content merely to adore Him with lip-service; we need to lower ourselves into a profound emptying out of self, and recognize that we are nothing, that we are less than nothing and, in this disposition, offer to the spotless Lamb who immolates Himself for the salvation of the world not only a sacrifice of adoration and of thanksgiving, but again a sacrifice of submission, of abandonment, and of consecration. Let us adhere to His divine will, detach ourselves from creatures, and renounce all human consolation, so as to live in Jesus only, and only for Jesus.

[7] Cf. Gal 2:20.
[8] Cf. Col 1:24.

We must never lose sight of our holy tabernacles: it is there that we find our strength and our virtue. If human infirmity and affairs allowed, we should pass our whole life at the feet of our divine Master. At least let us go there as often as possible, and quit so many futile occupations that rob us of precious time claimed for what we owe the love of a God.

Far from us be disgust, negligence, and frivolity. Alas! Is it possible that it should be burdensome for us to converse with our Sovereign Lord? Where is one better off than close to one's Father, to one's Spouse, to one's all? To live with Jesus—is this not to begin to live on earth the life that we are called to live in heaven? Ah! Can we say that we have faith if we complain of the length of time we spend before the Most Holy Sacrament?

What, however, does one see in the world, and perhaps even among us? Poor creatures, fragile nothings, worms of the earth, for whom it is such an effort to spend half an hour with the King of heaven and of earth! People consecrate days and nights to vain conversations, to futile entertainments, and always find too long the moments given to a God who forgets Himself for love of us. O heavens, be astonished! My Savior, *pardon them, for they know not what they do.*[9] *Happy*, says the Prophet, *are those who dwell in Your house, O Lord, and who praise you unceasingly.*[10] The saints understand this truth; how many there are who spent their days and nights with God, and who complained all the same of the rapid passage of time! So do the saints act and think, because they are quickened by a lively faith: let us have their faith, and we will think and act as they did.

All Christians ought to be in perpetual adoration before the Son of God in the Sacrament of the Altar. It is to make up for their coldness and indifference that the Institute was established. Let us carry out fervently so glorious a function and make of the

---

[9] Cf. Lk 23:34.
[10] Ps 83:5 [84:4].

altar our delights. Let our spirit and our body be bound thereto like two victims under the mastery of a pure and simple faith. If we are without taste for it, without light, without sensible consolation, we can, by the obscurity of our senses, render homage to this God who is hidden and brought to nothing. Let us abide before Him with patience, humility, and abandonment. Always it is for us a great honor to be able to keep watch with Jesus Christ.

If nearly all Christians are ungrateful towards this mystery of love, we, at least, will not be, and we will recognize the gift of God. One can say that the Eternal Father gives us, in our Institute, all that is most august of what He has; that He makes us the depositors and guardians of His most precious treasures. He gives us His divine Son, in whom He has placed all His good pleasure. This infinite gift He gave first of all to men, and they failed to recognize it. He sought souls who would know how to appreciate its value, and He chose us. May Jesus find abundantly in us the glory and the delight that others refuse Him elsewhere! May we, by our ardor, worthily repair for the coldness and impiety of so many others. Weep without ceasing over their ingratitude, and ask our heavenly Father to take pity on those who profane His divine Son. Even if the humiliations He endures in the Most Holy Sacrament of the Eucharist had occurred but one time, we should want to groan all our life long to make reparation for them. They are renewed every day; yes, every day, and in an infinity of places, Jesus Christ is the object of the most cutting outrages, of the most horrible sacrileges. What shall we do at the sight of so many crimes? My God, we ought to die of sorrow... Ah, at least, I will consecrate to You the rest of my life to repair, as best I can, Your glory, and to obtain of You that these cruel indignities to which You are exposed at last come to an end.

We must be ready at all times to die for the interests of Jesus the Host, and as we would never have the courage to sustain His interests at the price of our own blood if we do not begin to sustain them by death to ourselves, let us hold ourselves like victims always ready, and die ceaselessly to ourselves in all the occasions of sacrifice that present themselves. Let us begin by repairing in us the glory of our Savior by establishing His reign within us, and let us abandon ourselves to the justice of God so that He may make of us true daughters of the Holy Sacrament. Let us keep ourselves from putting obstacles in the way of His designs, and that we might begin to enter into them, let us break our hearts with a sincere contrition at the sight of our past infidelities, and cast ourselves into a profound abasement before the infinite Majesty of God.

All our life, let us thank Him for having chosen us to consecrate us to His Son in so special a manner. Let us not forget the obligations that this favor imposes, and let us fear that our grace be taken away from us to pass into more faithful hands. Before the altar, let us often examine if we are corresponding to our vocation. What a sad thing it would be if the Institute were to come to nothing by our fault and if Our Lord were deprived of the glory that He rightly expects of us. Let us make haste to enter into the usages of the precious quality of victimhood by a great simplicity of spirit, by a perfect obedience of heart and, above all, by a profound humility. Without humility, all our reparations would be no more than illusions.

Since Our Lord has made the Institute for us, since He has entrusted it to us, and since its progress and perfection depend on us, let us keep watch and pray. Take care lest we profane it rather than sanctify it. An exact account will be required of all our failings, of the graces of which we will have drawn no profit, and also of those which were destined for us, and of which we made ourselves unworthy. The account will be faithful, the judgment rigorous: think of that.

The Mass

At the morning's reading, which was about the focus we should have when attending the Holy Mass, Mother Mectilde said the following to us.

I CONFESS TO YOU, my Sisters, that I am amazed when I think that the Holy Sacrifice of the Mass, which is the greatest of all the mysteries of the Christian religion, is still so neglected and that we attend it with so little attention. We make a definite practice of going to Mass every day; I agree that this is good. This practice is holy and praiseworthy, but we do not go to Mass with the interior focus which must accompany such a holy thing. We say, "I am going to Mass." But what are you doing there? "Ah! I am going to assist at the death of a God."[1] We must, therefore, go with the dispositions of death. Yes, my Sisters, you may say in truth that you go to assist at the death of a God, for it is the same sacrifice which was offered once on the Cross with the shedding of blood. And although this offering is not bloody, it is nevertheless the same God who sacrifices Himself and is sacrificed there; it is He Himself who is the priest and the victim, for, observe that the priest, in the words of consecration, says, "This is *My* Body, this is *My* Blood." Therefore, it is Jesus Christ's place which he has at the altar. This holy and adorable Victim of the eternal Father offered Himself once in sacrifice on the tree of the Cross for all the sins of mankind, having poured out His precious Blood even to the last drop in order to pay the justice of His

---

[1] "Death of a God": a literary expression, based on the theological truth of the "communication of idioms" whereby that which pertains to Christ as man can be said of the divine Person, and vice versa.

divine Father for all our sins.[2] But as He cannot suffer again in this way through the shedding of His Blood, being glorious in heaven now, He offers Himself every day and at every moment on our altars through the hands of His priests, whom He established on earth to be our mediators, just as He is our Mediator in heaven before the eternal Father to obtain on our behalf pardon for our sins...

With what devotion do you think the most holy Virgin assisted at the Holy Mass celebrated by the Apostles in her sacred presence after the Ascension of her divine Son and their adorable Master? What was the quality of her inner attention toward this precious sacrifice, which she knew to be the true re-presentation[3] of the one she had seen offered once on the Cross by the shedding of all His Blood?...

Again, what was the quality of her inner attention at seeing Him immolated anew in an unbloody manner, but in a manner which is more able to win our hearts, since it is love alone which keeps Him on our altars to fill us with graces?...

Therefore, let us turn to the most holy Mother of God and pray to her that we may have a share in her interior attention when assisting at the Holy Sacrifice of the Mass, and in the dispositions she had at Communion. She will not refuse them to us, if we ask them of her with humility and confidence. Let us pray to her, then, that she may prepare us to receive her divine Son, or rather, that she may come into us herself to prepare a place for Him in our hearts (as she knows that our hearts should be given to Him), and adorn them with all the virtues and dispositions

---

[2] Heb 9:14.

[3] The Mass—and the liturgy in general—make the mysteries of Christ present anew, even as for the Hebrews, remembrance or memorial meant the making-present of the power of that which is recalled. The Church is not just "presenting" the mysteries as a teacher presents a lesson in a classroom, but delivering them and their graces to us mystically.

that will please Him, so that she may make us worthy to possess Jesus Christ through this adorable mystery. One can say she has the power to give Jesus Christ to souls, since she received Him first from the eternal Father, who made that great gift through her, in order to give Him to the world.

We should receive Communion only so that we may put our Communion into her hallowed hands, that she may use it to the glory of her divine Son, that she may offer it to Him, and that it may be pleasing to Him. Let us pray to this mother of goodness that she will obtain for us, in her mercy, that all our Communions, so frequent, may be full of a holiness which honors God; that she will grant us the favor of making a holy use of them as Jesus Christ expects and requires of us, making us live more from His life and from His virtues, in order to put them into practice continually in all our actions. Finally, let us pray that she will make Him reign in our hearts as she made Him reign in hers. If we ask her for this favor, she will grant it to us, since she is all-powerful in heaven as well as on earth, and her divine Son has put into her hands all the graces that He wants to grant.

n. 14, Conversation on Holy Mass, October 27, 1694

Everything in the Holy Sacrifice of the Mass is infinite. The victim offered is the Son of God, a Person of infinite merit. This divine Son is sacrificed for the glory of God His Father, infinite in all His perfections, God offered to God. This infinite Son is the first and primary priest and celebrant who offers Himself to His Father in His own person by the hands of the priest. It is He who by the mouth of His minister pronounces the sacramental words that accomplish this great mystery: "This is My Body." That is why, in Psalm 109, He is called by His Father "eternal priest."[4] This infinite Son sacrifices Himself in a way that is utterly perfect and beyond human understanding. This is why a single Mass,

---

[4] Ps 109 [110]:4.

even one celebrated by a wicked priest, gives more glory to God than all the praises of men and angels...

My sisters, I regard the Holy Sacrifice of the Mass as the most magnificent feast, for in it we eat the flesh of the Son of God and we drink His Blood, so that the guests' souls are completely filled with Jesus Christ. Consider: we are filled with His divinity and His humanity, with His holy soul and all His infinite perfections and, by concomitance, with the Father and the Holy Spirit. This is what is offered in this precious mystery, which being too common is neglected and being so excellent is still understood only by a few...

And we have an absolute obligation to apply to ourselves the command which Our Lord tells us by the mouth of His priest: *Quotiescumque feceritis, in mei memoriam facietis.*[5] Therefore, we must renew this sorrowful mystery; it is His intention, and the reason He instituted the sacrifice of the altar.[6] He wants to renew it every day before His Father, in order to restore the glory which our sins have stolen from Him and to make satisfaction to His offended justice. He renews it also within our hearts to light a new flame of His love in them, for it is the infinite love He has for

---

[5] As often as ye shall do these things, ye shall do them in remembrance of me (cf. Lk 22:19, 1 Cor 11:24). Mother Mectilde refers to the words spoken at the conclusion of the consecration of the chalice in the traditional Roman rite of Mass. In the rite of Paul VI, they are replaced with the words *Hoc facite in meam commemorationem*, Do this in remembrance of me.

[6] "The Eucharist is a constant presence—an insertion in each moment of history—of the unique saving act accomplished by Christ. It is the constant presence of this definitive act in the life of the Church and the life of each Christian. It is through the Eucharist that Christ never ceases to capture the Church, and in her, every Christian, in the grace of that unique saving act. Only in this perspective can we comprehend the plenitude of meaning and the profundity of the bond with which we are joined to Christ in Eucharistic Communion. He becomes not only our food, He makes us enter into His sacrifice with Him. In the sacrificial meal, in fact, those who have presented the victim as a sign of their own offering and consecration to God feed on

us that keeps Him in subjection and makes Him obey so punctually the voice of the priest when he says, *Hoc est Corpus meum.*[7]

What a sight to see Jesus on the altar, immolated as truly as on Calvary, saying to us with the voice of His outpoured blood, "I die and I sacrifice myself anew at every hour and at every moment for you"—and can you think of anything else than that infinite love, taking away His life?

n. 1836

In order to attend Mass well, I know of nothing better than to see Jesus Christ in the person of the priest in all that he does and all that he says...

The same sacrifice of Calvary is renewed every day at the altar in an unbloody manner, and it is no less wonderful, since in it He gives to God His Father an infinite glory on our behalf; He intercedes for us; He asks mercy for us; He atones for us and immolates Himself for us... Therefore, we must unite ourselves to all that is said and all that is done to merit our salvation by Jesus Christ (represented by the priest) as Mediator in the service of God His Father. You know, my Sisters, as I have told you before, that we participate in the sacrifice of Jesus Christ, our divine Head, as members of His mystical Body. The rest of the time, we must remain in reverence and in adoration, up to the time of Holy Communion, uniting ourselves to the angels and blessed

---

that victim in order to participate in its consecration, in order to enter more profoundly into union with it in its state of consecrated victimhood. To celebrate the Eucharist at Mass and to receive Communion there is to ratify the offering that Christ made of ourselves, offering us with Him in offering Himself so that in Him reconciled humanity might be consecrated to His Father" (Dom Georges Lefebvre, *Dieu présent*, DDB, 1978).

[7] Lk 22:19, Mt 26: 26–28, Mk 14:22–24. Again, Mother Mectilde refers to the formula of the consecration of the Host in the traditional Roman rite, which is simply: *Hoc est enim Corpus meum.*

souls, who offer homage and marvel at the love that God has for His creatures in this august mystery...

We must also prepare ourselves to receive Communion along with the priest (or spiritually) by a burning desire to be united to Jesus Christ, praying that He will draw us to Himself and that we may be entirely buried in Him. So, let us sink entirely into Him and remain in Him. Through the Holy Mass we have passed into Jesus Christ and He passes into us in order to communicate His divine life to us, to make us live the life of God.

We must pray to Him to hide us in Himself, so that we may be renewed and live no longer except from His Spirit, since it is the principal effect of the Holy Mass to draw us to Jesus Christ and to unite us completely to Him.

A nun asked our worthy Mother how we were to be sacrificed with Jesus Christ. She answered: "As members united to their Head."

n. 2192, Informal Conversations

Not only must I explain to you Jesus offered to His Father as a victim for the sins of the world, I must also introduce to you the continual effects of this state. It is true that He said His first Mass today in the Temple[8] and that He glorified His Father infinitely by His immolation. But He is also *our* Host and *our* Priest: He is the High Priest according to the Order of Melchisedech; we are presented to the Father, by Him and with Him, or rather, we form only a single victim, being in Him as members united to their head, and all that He does in this adorable action, He did for us.

n. 1065, Letter on the Presentation of Jesus in the Temple

In the Mass, all the mysteries of Jesus Christ Our Lord are represented to us. A soul who is a little enlightened finds there all

---

[8] Mother Mectilde means that it was at His circumcision that He first offered Himself by the shedding of His Blood.

the dispositions with which He acted and suffered during the course of His holy life. The Mass is an ineffable mystery in which the eternal Father receives infinite homage: in it He is adored, loved, and praised as much as He deserves; and that is why we are advised to receive Communion frequently, in order to render to God, through Jesus, all the duties we owe Him. This is impossible without Jesus Christ who comes into us in order to accomplish [in us] the same sacrifice as that of the Holy Mass. We must receive Communion in a spirit of death, and in that way we fulfill what is said to us in the Gospel, "Do this is in memory of Me,"[9] in memory of My death. We must, therefore, bring to Communion an intention of death, so that we allow Jesus alone to accomplish His divine sacrifice.

n. 2634, *Informal Conversations*

I have the custom of commemorating every year, on this day, the holy desires of the adorable Heart of Jesus, following the words which the Church presents to us in the Divine Office: *Desiderio desideravi.*[10] It is through these words that Jesus expresses His infinite desires to give Himself to men, to attract and unite them to Himself. I have been occupied this whole day in adoring and admiring the loving desires of Jesus and considering why He wanted to give Himself to men through the institution of the Sacrament of His adorable Body before suffering for them and why He gave His Body and Blood only to the twelve Apostles and not to the many disciples and holy women who were following Him.

I saw that the reason was that Jesus Christ, by giving them Communion with His holy hands, imparted to the Apostles His grace and a source of grace to be communicated to all men and, as head [of the mystical body], He united them all to Himself in

[9] Lk 22:19.
[10] Lk 22:15. With desire have I desired (to eat this pasch with you).

their persons, so that they could be the foundation of His Church and the leaders and heralds by which the Gospel was to be carried through the whole world. I saw also that the reason why He instituted our divine Sacrament before suffering His Passion (for He could have done it in His agony, or on the Cross) was, in virtue of His holy Body and His precious Blood which He gave to His Apostles, to unite them to His divine Person, and, in them, all men, so as to make them a single offering with Him in the sacrifice that He was going to make of Himself, so that they would suffer everything with Him and would merit by this union the strength and grace to bear all kinds of pains and sufferings, each one according to his state.

n. 682, Conference for Holy Thursday

Frequent Communion

A LLOW ME TO SAY that you remain too burdened and that you listen to too much evil. You have not come back enough to God. Do you not know that it is only His goodness that can protect you, and that nothing is to be hoped except through His most holy Mother, who can obtain everything you need? You do not take enough strength from her. Frequent Communion is absolutely necessary for you, and you do not receive often enough.[1] You drown and sink yourself in thought, and this is not where you will find strength and the remedy [for your ills]. It is good to have recourse to God and receive Him. You must no longer refrain from it [Communion] if you do not want to be endlessly lost. Where can you get knowledge other than from that divine Sacrament? And the grace to act as He desires, in the spirit of this divine Jesus? You can have this only in frequent Communion, and your heart should long only for this Eucharistic bread. You feel your need sufficiently. I assure you that God desires this of you, and that if you are faithful to it,

---

[1] The situation in which Mother Mectilde was writing about "frequent Communion" is very different from that of the Catholic Church after the Second Vatican Council. From the time of the early Middle Ages, reception of Communion by laity had tended to become infrequent, ranging from once a year (the obligatory minimum) to once a month, or, in special cases, weekly. Religious could obtain permission from their spiritual directors to receive more often. At the start of the twentieth century, St. Pius X encouraged frequent Communion for reasons akin to those given by Mother Mectilde. Both, of course, emphasize the conditions requisite for communicating fruitfully.

you will receive the effects of grace which are beyond words. With the same heart with which I desire these [graces] for you, I am, with all respect...

n. 2464, to the Duchess of Orléans

Begin to receive Communion on all Saturdays and feasts in order never to stop. I will never have any consolation unless I see your soul possessed of this holy practice, whatever favor you have shown me by honoring me with your friendship. I ask this of you with as much earnestness as someone aspiring to the highest good fortune. And I dare to say that I ask it on behalf of my God who desires this of you. He wants to come to you and nevertheless you do not receive Him. You have many small weaknesses that will be eradicated only by availing yourself of this Eucharistic bread. Why deprive your soul of an infinite good? Listen to the voice of this marvelous Savior who calls from the depth of your heart, *"Aperi, aperi, mihi soror, mea sponsa.*[2] Open to Me, open to Me, My sister, My bride, My beloved, your heart, that I may make My eternal dwelling in it and take My rest in you." He wants to be united to you, in order to make you entirely one with Him. Do not refuse that which the angels consider themselves infinitely blessed and unworthy to receive. Surely, if you do not listen to this divine voice I will be a thousand times more aggrieved than if I were condemned to death. I see the moments passing, the weeks and months, and, by I do not know what temptation, you delay your eternal happiness. I beg you not to go on any longer like this, for fear that, when you desire to receive Communion, you are no longer able; and meanwhile you deprive your soul of the divine life.

Pardon, Madam, for I confess my boldness to you. However, I do not promise that I will correct myself, since I have too much

[2] Cf. Song 5:2.

affection for your soul. It is too dear and too precious to me not to wish fervently for you the greatest good your soul could ever have.

n. 1580, to the Duchess of Orléans

My desire would be to see you receive Communion often, and if your confessor will allow you to receive this grace tomorrow, I urge you to take advantage of it. You cannot give yourself too much to Jesus Christ, nor can you surrender too much to His intentions to possess you through this adorable Sacrament. You need to drown your weakness in His divine power and in the desire to be completely filled with Him.

"As I live for My Father," says Jesus Christ, "so all those who receive Me live for Me."[3] O blessed life, to live for Jesus Christ and from Jesus Christ, to be nourished and sustained by Him! This is why He is in the Host and will be there until the end of the world. And His desire is to be received *now*, so that He may continually work the effects of His love and His mercy, that He might live in us and we in Him—in short, that we be transformed in His love, being completely engulfed in the divinity and made absolutely one with Jesus Christ. It seems to me that a soul who communicates frequently receives a great deal more strength, grace, and blessing than those who refrain.

Let us go to God with humility and trust. He is good with an infinite goodness. He knows our weakness and our incapacity; He will make up for it with His divine sufficiency. Oh! When will we belong entirely to Jesus, our hearts longing only for His love, and living with His life, and permeated with His consciousness? Let us give ourselves to His eternal desire to possess us for this. How sorrowful and unbearable this life is without the love of Jesus and without being on the Cross for Him!

n. 1697, to the Countess of Châteauvieux

---

[3] Cf. Jn 6:57.

I dare to promise you that Jesus is with you, hidden in the depths of your heart... Do your utmost to not abstain from taking Communion. You must go to God for Himself, so that He may come into you to fight for His interests Himself. You are not capable of sustaining them. Take heart, do not be discouraged!

n. 1434, to a nun, rue Cassette

There is no doubt that you did badly by not going to Communion on Monday. This infidelity brought the others along with it. It was necessary to be restrained on these holy days, especially in the mornings, in order to prepare for the time of Communion; but since you have been weak, you must resolve to bear, in a spirit of penance, the shame and bewilderment you feel. I order you, as much as Our Lord gives me the power, to remove yourself as much as possible from creatures, for these three days that remain—without, however, neglecting your family, according to your duties.

n. 599, to a person in the world

It is not enough to know that you must go to Holy Communion. It is necessary to endeavor to have the grace of communicating often. And supposing that you were to persist in your present state, there is a temptation to refrain, under the pretext of seeing yourself little disposed to receive it. Go to God with trust and love, do not deprive yourself of Him out of fear. Alas! What presumption to think that we are able to prepare for Communion! It is God alone who can prepare us by His graces and His mercies. Accordingly, you have nothing and can do nothing unless God gives it to you. Present yourself to Him so that you may receive what He desires to give you, and ask Jesus to receive Himself in you and to glorify Himself there, since you are incapable of being able to do this well. Let His love supply for everything. And in this simple disposition, receive Communion often.

n. 530, to the Countess of Châteauvieux

You must go to Communion as often as the community does, unless some infirmity hinders you. You should never deprive yourself of it through your own reasoning...

You will act in a holy way by renewing yourself often and not following your fears and your aversions towards Holy Communion and prayer. Have more love than fear. I am delighted to see you with the feeling of gratitude for God's gifts to you. I implore you, my child, to spend your whole life in a love of humble gratitude, giving thanks to God, praising and blessing Him for all His gifts. It is a holy practice wherein I have found miracles and very singular increases in grace. By giving thanks to Our Lord, you draw down new blessings.

n. 301, to a nun, rue Cassette

I know very well that your needs are great and that you have an absolute necessity to communicate more frequently than Providence and obedience require you to do; but this must not make you lose the reverence you owe to Jesus Christ. That is why you must learn to receive Communion out of love for Him, for His interests, and not for yours; because in communicating so frequently and for our own interests, there is a danger of communicating unworthily or through self-love...

When you do not have enough time and when business or charity towards your neighbor or obedience employs you elsewhere, obviously you go by God's command, who wills to keep you from actual Communion: but you can always make a spiritual Communion, and you should put this into practice, because souls who are faithful in this make very good progress.

n. 609, Essay

With regard to your frequent Communions, it is not that I cease to wish you were at liberty to do this more often; but since your duties keep you captive, sacrifice yourself and endure this privation, being content to do as you have been accustomed. The anxiety in which your mind finds itself because of your many duties and your lack of leisure takes away from you the unction of your Communions. I think that you should wait until you are more free to make them more frequent. Above all things, I entreat you never to cease to be faithful to God and to abandon everything to Him, to detach yourself from your own interests and perform all your actions according to the order of the divine will, receiving everything from His holy hand. Surrender all your affairs to Him, never losing confidence in His goodness, whatever difficulties or reversals befall you.

n. 1869, to the Countess of Rochefort

I received a new attraction to Holy Communion, and because I have sometimes refrained through fear, I have resumed for love, it seems to me, and I desire to receive Communion in order to enter totally anew into Jesus Christ and to live from His Life and His Spirit.

n. 1807, to Jean de Bernières, June 25, 1648

Have courage and patience: I do not restrict your Communions. You should go as much as you can; do not worry about your mind, and do not give in to your discouragement. God has more goodness for you than you have malice; lose yourself in faith.

n. 818, to Mother St. Placid, rue St. Louis, Paris

I am anxious about the dear Mother Subprioress who is said to be ill. I ask you to assure her of my most tender affection. I would have more desire to talk with her, but it must wait still a little while, and, while waiting, I ask you to tell her that the penance we order for her is to receive Communion more frequently, rising above the impressions she feels.

n. 1787, to Mother St. Gertrude, Mistress of Novices,
November 9, 1695

Dearest, this will be a single little word for your retreat: you must receive Communion every day, but do not go to Confession every day for this.

n. 168, *to Mother St. Placid*

Keep your peace in your precious abandonment and remember me before Our Lord. Continue to receive Communion every day.

n. 922, *to Mother Gertrude of St. Opportune*

It is astonishing to see the goodness of a God always ready to give Himself every time we desire to receive Communion. He never refuses. Go to Communion every day; He will come.

n. 3150, *Conference for the Saturday of First Week of Lent*

Virtues Drawn
from Jesus Christ

TERTULLIAN SAID that our soul is Christian, but he did not say that our nature is. St. Paul laments, saying that he felt "a law in himself which is contrary to the law of God."[1] Assuredly, this great Apostle was experiencing the burden of Adam in himself. Everyone has in himself the ground of sin, which we have inherited from Adam; it is only the most holy Virgin, the Mother of God, who has been preserved from it.

It is good and very beneficial to understand the sinful ground that is in us. As for myself, I attribute to Holy Communion the fact that we do not fall into continual disorders. It is necessary give thanks to God for this at every hour, if it were possible, and meanwhile remain in a holy contempt of ourselves and a sincere confidence in God's goodness.

n. 611, to Mother St. Placid, Paris, October 30, 1691

You come to receive Our Lord in Holy Communion, my Sisters. I ask you, tell me the effect it produced in each one of you and what Our Lord said to you in the depths of your heart... What does He say to you in the depths of your soul? What do you hear? "This is my beloved Son, hear Him."[2] It is His Word that He sent to the earth, and we find no other commandment spoken by the Father than to listen to His Son. "Hear Him." It is He who

[1] Rm 7:23.
[2] Mt 17:5.

instructs us in the duties of our salvation. "Hear Him." What prevents you from hearing Him? The noise of creatures, an insolent imagination, a dissipated mind, senses which are not mortified.

There must be a great quiet in our interior, where our divine Savior does not fail to instruct us, although we do not listen to Him [as we should]. If He keeps silence sometimes, we should remain in His holy presence in reverence and adoration...

He speaks today on Mount Tabor about the excess of His sufferings;[3] He teaches us that it is necessary to suffer before entering into glory.[4] If He causes a sample of His glory to shine forth, it is in conversing about His sufferings.

I greatly fear that we have not made good use of our Communions and that we go to them through habit and negligently. God will require an account of it on the day of judgment. One ought to see only Jesus Christ in us; we have received Him so many times. However, we are always in ourselves and for ourselves. His intention is to make us live with His life.

n. 3150, Conference for the Saturday of the first week of Lent

Each day that you have the good fortune to receive Communion, it is necessary to have the intention to honor Our Lord in one of the titles He has with respect to us—King, father, teacher, shepherd, judge, doctor, friend, and spouse—or other times, to honor His virtues...

The day that is a feast of a saint, receive Communion under his patronage and protection, offering Our Lord the honor which the saint has given to Him, in order to make up for what you fail

---

[3] In the ancient liturgical calendar, the Gospel for the Saturday of the First Week of Lent is the same as that for the First Sunday of Lent, namely, the Transfiguration in St. Matthew's account (17:1–9). However, Mother Mectilde refers to a phrase in St. Luke's account, where he says Jesus, Moses, and Elias "dicebant excessum ejus, quem completurus erat in Jerusalem" (Lk 9:31).

[4] Cf. Lk 24:26.

to give Him, and at the same time ask the saint to obtain by his intercession the graces you need and the virtues in which he excelled. Give thanks to God for the mercies He has poured out on the saint's life and the glory to which He raised him in heaven, where he is, rejoicing in His divine presence.

n. 4, Essay

Jesus Christ crucified and sanctified is the science of the saints. We find in Him the lights and knowledge which are necessary for us. *Accedite ad eum et illuminamini*.[5] Let us draw near to Him, and we will be enlightened. This divine Savior says no word in the Host. Nevertheless, He still acts as teacher and master. One saint said that "the Cross was the pulpit of this dying teacher." We can say the same of the Holy Eucharist, where He speaks to our soul, provided that our soul is attentive. The states He bears in this august mystery are so many lessons that He gives us to conform us to them and to make us live from the Eucharistic life... And if we examine as thoroughly as is necessary the mystery of God's infinite charity, we will see there in a state of death[6] the One who is the Word and the Wisdom of the Father abiding in perpetual silence; the One whose immensity fills the heavens and the earth, contained in the smallest particle of the Host. We will see that the Sovereign and the Almighty who governs all things obeys a priest, who makes Him descend from

[5] Ps 33:6 [34:5]. Come to Him and be enlightened.

[6] According to St. Thomas Aquinas, the Lord of glory present under the consecrated species is the Christ-who-suffered, *Christus passus*. In the *Commentary on John*, he writes: "Since this sacrament is of the Lord's Passion, it contains within itself Christ who suffered. Hence whatever is an effect of the Lord's Passion is wholly contained in this sacrament, for it is nothing else than the application of the Lord's Passion to us. . . . Hence it is clear that the destruction of death, which Christ accomplished by his death, and the restoration of life, which he accomplished by his resurrection, are effects of this sacrament" (*Super Ioan.* 6, lec. 6, §964; cf. *In IV Sent.*, d. 8, q. 1, a. 2, qa. 2; *ST* III, q. 66, a. 9, ad 5 and q. 73, a. 5, ad 2).

Heaven to be reduced to such a humble state. O prodigy! O miracle of love! It is indeed in this adorable mystery that He is truly, according to the expression of Scripture, "the hidden God."[7]

Journée Religieuse: Writings on Thursday

Mother Mectilde said the following to the lay Sisters: "In order to accustom ourselves to keeping silence, we would need to do what was done by a great saint. He put a stone in his mouth to remind himself never to speak any useless words. It would be necessary for us to do the same thing to refrain from saying words that offend God and wound charity. I do not know of anything more surprising than the tongue, which is so often honored by contact with Jesus Christ, which has the first honor of welcoming Him, and which, in some way, may do what it wants with Him, since it is free to keep and then to consume the sacred Host. (However, the holy Fathers are not of this opinion, saying that, for Communion, we must chew, and that only when the Host passes from the mouth to the stomach is it received by the heart.) I say! This tongue, which has the happiness to receive its God, so great, so adorable, so incomprehensible, with all His divine perfections, all His gifts and graces, which receives Jesus Christ with all His holiness, His virtues, and His merits, who applies to it His precious Blood and all that He did and suffered for its salvation, who brings to it His humility, his patience, His meekness, and all His other virtues—what do you want greater than that? It is not the saints' virtues He gives you, but His virtues in Himself, who practiced them to give you the example; it is His sanctity that He brings you in order to sanctify you. I say! All these infinite graces do not have the power to prevent us from saying words that offend this God of goodness and require us to be mortified. I have never known a better way to destroy the passions than Holy Communion, and when frequent Com-

---

[7] Is 45:15.

munions do not have the power to humble them, in truth, I assure you that I do not believe there is anything else we can turn to. What! God in Himself, in His divine power, will not have this power over us, who ennothings Himself even to the level of the corruption of our being and who reduces Himself to the lowest humiliations! Oh! My Sisters, it is shocking! I know souls who have received many insults and injuries, and going to Communion on that account, at the coming of Our Lord, all the resentment and pain which they experienced vanished, so much power has Holy Communion over holy souls. I ask you to consider this."

Catherine de Bar, Fondation de Rouen, *Rouen* 1977, p. 67

For a soul in the state of grace, the good effects that suffering produces are beyond understanding. I adore my God who accomplishes His work in you this way. Nevertheless I pray to Him to strengthen you to recover soon. I am sorry you are deprived of Holy Communion for so long a time, but this arrangement [of affairs] is connected to the other arrangements; it is the time of pure and universal deprivation.

n. 1376, *to Madam de Béthune, September* 29, 1686

Alas! If wishes had a place, I would exempt you entirely from all the ills with which I see you burdened. I suffer them with you, I carry them along with your dear person to Holy Communion in order to obtain grace and strength for you.

n. 449, *to Madam de Béthune, November* 5, 1686

Remember that you were never more a victim than you are at present. Our Lord will sustain you and restore you. Take heart. All your strength and your life is in Jesus Christ and, through Him, in His most holy Mother. If you had been here, you would not have passed one day without receiving that divine Bread. I know indeed that it is only this which sustains you.

n. 2955, *to Madam de Béthune, September* 27, 1686

On every side you will find the Cross; all creatures will be for you causes of it. This is your destiny, it is your lot—but a happy lot in the divine light and truth. What happiness to have so much resemblance to and connection with Jesus Christ! I know very well that nature does not hear this language and that it suffers cruelly, but I hope that through Holy Communion your body will be strengthened and will be made able to endure everything by the divine power which was communicated to the holy humanity of Jesus Christ.

n. 793, to Madam de Béthune, September 25, 1684

The mercies of God are so excessive in your case that they cause me astonishment and wonder. Behold the fruits of the Most Holy Sacrament and the purpose for which this God, who is all love, Jesus Christ, has placed Himself in the Holy Eucharist. There is nothing to say about what you wrote to me except that you must burn with love and humble gratitude, that you must be very faithful in order to give Jesus Christ the joy of possessing you entirely, without any division, but purely.

n. 2405, to a nun of Toul

May Jesus, ennothinged in His divine Sacrament, bring about in us the perfection of holy and complete ennothingment.

n. 842, to M. Roquelay, February 22, 1653

The poverties and darkness that one experiences in Holy Communion are not always chastisements for the infidelities of a soul. No, it is often the action of God, who wants to purify the soul by means of this privation and poverty; and although it seems to the soul that some Communions are unworthy and defective, they are still very precious in the eyes of God, who does not fail to work in the depths of that soul and sanctify it, although it sees and feels nothing.

n. 2071, Essay

Present to His adorable Majesty one small moment of your sufferings, and pray that, by virtue of the Precious Blood of Jesus, it may be applied to my soul to obtain the grace of purity and fidelity to the pure and simple loving regard of God. I am having prayers said for you.

n. 1267, to Jean de Bernières, October 23, 1646

We must beware of discouragement, for the majority of souls fall into it saying: "For such a long time have I attended Mass and offered my imperfections, and I still have them all and I am not dead to the least of them." Others say: "I have received Communion so many times and I am not at all transformed into Jesus Christ, which is the effect of Holy Communion; therefore it is not necessary to receive Communion anymore." No, no, there is something you must note: it is in order to have us hear Mass often and receive Communion many times that Jesus Christ does not effect this complete death or total transformation. Instead, He leaves us our imperfections so that we may make a continual sacrifice of them in combating them constantly for Him. This is why Our Lord does not cause this [transformation] all at once; these matters for battle He leaves for the sake of our fidelity.

n. 2357, Essay on Holy Mass

Our Lord Jesus Christ alone can adore God perfectly in spirit and in truth, and we can do it only by union with Him.

We are most united to Him after receiving Holy Communion. At that time, He draws our entire substance to Himself. Oh! If we could see the wonders which He works in a person who receives Communion! The person is then completely transformed into Jesus Christ: eyes, hands, the entire body and soul, everything is Jesus Christ.

Jesus Christ adores God in the person, and the person adores God through Jesus Christ, and this adoration can continue for as long as we desire. Oh! If you knew the gift which God gives you through Holy Communion! Jesus is all yours, His Body, His Soul, His Divinity, all His Blood, His sufferings, and His infinite merits, all this is given for your use; you will be asked to give an account of it.

You receive Communion frequently; very good. I will rejoice in this, but let it be done worthily. Our Lord, in coming to you, brings to you His humility, His charity, His meekness, and all His virtues; live then, from His spirit, and may His virtues be seen in you.

You can adore God everywhere. He is in you. Walk in His holy presence and you will see that you will do all things well.

n. 315, Conference on Holy Communion

I just received Holy Communion, wherein I have received so many mercies from Our Lord's unspeakable goodness which I cannot express! Oh! how good God is! Oh! how good God is, with an infinite goodness! Oh happy and a thousand times happy is the soul who has the grace and honor to be perfectly God's. It is not the ecstasies or revelations I have received that I cherish, but more His mercies, since they bind me more purely and powerfully to God.

n. 1575, to the Countess of Châteauvieux

The holy Gospel which the Church presents to us today[8] is so rich that I do not know where to start. It is an abyss in which I am lost. But because there are so many truths contained in it— and this would cause me to make a long discourse—I will confine myself to the consideration of the marriage which Jesus Christ wants to contract with your soul, without dwelling on the one which He makes with human nature.

I see that the divine Savior is taken with such great love for your soul that He wants, without consideration for His greatness

---

[8] Mt 22:1–14, read for the Nineteenth Sunday after Pentecost.

and your lowliness, to enter into this sacred marriage, and it is for this reason that He descended from Heaven and has come to commune with us, not only by the mystery of the Incarnation, but in the adorable Eucharist. I see Jesus Christ, the only Son of the Eternal Father, loving your soul passionately. I see Him opening Himself to an infinity of pains, insults, poverties, and contempt, in order to put Himself in a state to enter into this divine marriage. Tomorrow, consequently, is the marriage of your soul; and you must solemnize this precious alliance and be careful of refusing to give yourself to this mystical feast in any way...

Where is the banquet of this royal wedding held? In the depths of your soul, which is a magnificent palace which the heavenly King has adorned with His wonderful treasures, which are His divine virtues, gifts, and mercies. There is an abundance of all the mercies and graces of Jesus Christ the Bridegroom, which He gives to your soul as a gift. The witnesses of that sacred marriage are the divine Persons, the Father, the Holy Spirit, and the Eternal Word, who, speaking to your soul, utter this mysterious word, found in the Holy Scriptures, "I espouse you to me in faith."[9] This reality is so deep and so true that you never receive Communion without this sacred marriage being renewed.

Consider, therefore, in what manner you should conduct yourself at such a solemnity, so advantageous to your soul and elevating it to a dignity so precious. Take care never to refuse to attend this delightful wedding; take care that your heart does not behave like the wicked people in the Gospel, who preferred the things of earth to the divine banquet, or like the others who killed the servants of the king, who went to invite them on his behalf. Never stifle the movements of grace; prefer nothing to the love of Jesus Christ.

And beware of attending Mass without your wedding garment, which denotes purity of heart and detachment from all

---

[9] Hos 2:20.

creatures, which indeed includes holiness of life and purity of intention. Let us do all things in harmony with the divine will. This intention keeps our soul separate from all that is not God and beautifies it with Jesus Christ's holy dispositions. And, for this reason, she is adorned with the wedding garment and capable of being admitted to the sublime and magnificent banquet where she is filled with God Himself, with such abundance that the soul which has partaken even once as she should, with the necessary dispositions, will never more hunger for the things of earth. Oh! May the soul who in faith consumes Jesus Christ in the sacred Host truly understand what I say. All creatures become insipid to her, and she can no longer take any delight except in enjoying Jesus her spouse, whom she finds "better than wine."[10]

n. 2040, *to the Countess of Châteauvieux*

[10] Song 1:2.

Dispositions for Holy Communion

MAY YOUR PRIMARY MOTIVE for Holy Communion be to give yourself to Jesus, to give Him the freedom to do in you everything which is in accordance with His good pleasure, without considering yourself or your own perfection. In your past life, you lived and received Communion so much for yourself; from now on, live and receive Communion only for Jesus, for His pleasure, for His designs, and for His intentions. Receive Communion to cling to the design and desire which He has to see you completely His, to see His love reign in you, to be united to Him and to become one single thing with Him.

n. 530, to the Countess of Châteauvieux

Our intentions for Holy Communion should be to do what God desires of us and to sacrifice ourselves to this adorable will, which should be our rule, our strength, our light, our fervor, and our perfection, and to bind ourselves to this as closely as we can.

n. 551, Conference for the night vigil of Christmas

Receive Communion for Jesus and not for yourself, for His intentions and for His satisfaction only.

n. 2227, to Mother Marie de Jésus Chopinel, rue St. Louis, Paris

I bid you to receive Communion in order to abandon yourself to His power, and not to seek in yourself for what is not there; you will find everything in Jesus Christ. Let us wait in patience and humble submission. Say an *Ave Maria* before Holy Communion.

n. 1658, to a nun, rue Cassette

I believe it is your intention to receive Communion today; try not to miss it, and if you do not find all the devotion that you would like in this divine and holy action, humble yourself in order to make up for it. Make the effort to unite yourself ceaselessly to Jesus Christ who is your blessed center; outside of Him there is only bitterness, sorrow, vanity, and the trickery of the human mind!

n. 133, to the Countess of Rochefort, June 5, 1659

Regarding your Communions, I advise you not to miss them voluntarily and not to follow your own will in this. Under the pretext of your coldness and indifference, you weaken your soul which cannot be sustained except by the grace of Holy Communion. The more often you refrain, the less you will want to communicate. Beyond this, you would be unfaithful by refraining on your own account. Where will you go to draw the strength to fight and to conquer your enemies if not from Jesus Christ in the divine Communion?

Go to Communion with humble confidence in the goodness of Our Lord, who ushered into His banquet the halt, the maimed, in short, the most wretched. We have the life of grace only in Jesus Christ and through Jesus Christ. Therefore, we must go to Him, to bring Him our miseries—we have only these to give Him—everything else is from Him. But our miseries, our weaknesses, and our sins, these are what is from us. And this is what the Lord wants us to give Him.

n. 396, to Mother St. Placid, rue St. Louis, Paris

It is necessary to prepare yourself for Holy Communion according to your small ability, but if your mind runs away like an escaped horse, do not be troubled; it is a beast, do not follow it. St. Teresa [of Avila] suffered from this trouble for long years. It is enough from time to time for us to renew ourselves in faith by an act of adoration towards Jesus Christ...

Continue to receive Communion. It is sufficient that you unite your intentions to those of Jesus, of His most holy Mother, and of the Church. Do not believe that you are able to do nothing; Our Lord will not be profaned in you if you receive Communion simply as I tell you, in order to give yourself to Him and that He may do with you according to His intention and not according to your thinking. Be truly little, then, and do not be surprised by your sins; on the contrary, you should be surprised at the goodness of God, who prevents you from doing worse—and give thanks for it. When you no longer strain yourself to have the concentration you desire in your Communions, your mind will be healed without thinking about it. Practice patience in the midst of your interior poverty, remain at peace, and pray to God for us.

n. 32, to Mother St. Francis of Paola, rue St. Louis, Paris

The Christian soul should not communicate for her own interests, but only out of reverence for Jesus Christ. Do not have any other intentions than His, so that He alone will reign in your soul, so that He will be glorified there, so that He will have life in you, and so that you will have Him in all your life's actions.

n. 609, Essay on Communion

Let us burn with the divine fire that so often comes into us! When we receive Communion, we have no excuse, since we find in this divine Sacrament the strength to overcome ourselves and the life we need for the service of God; we find there everything we can desire. You received Communion today and you complain that you do not burn with divine fire? What! God gives Himself to you, He gives you Himself utterly, and you remain in coldness and indifference—you are not absolutely burning with His love, you are not totally pierced with gratitude for so great a blessing?

Ah! Do not neglect so precious a gift! When you go to Communion, it is necessary to bring to Our Lord the passion that dominates you, whether it be pride, anger, or something else, begging Him to destroy it. Always have recourse to God; say to Him with confidence, "Lord, I come to You who are my strength, because I am only weakness, I can do nothing without You. Help me by Your grace; destroy in me what displeases You."

I have observed that, although we may be recollected during the time in advance of Holy Communion and during Holy Mass, ten or fifteen minutes before Communion we become distracted and lukewarm, we lose our interior concentration, so that we are never more distracted and interiorly colder than when we go to Communion. This is painful, and it is the devil who causes it in order to deprive us of the great goods that inner attention and fervor would bring us. Do not be anxious about it, but make an effort not to allow yourself to become distracted and lukewarm through negligence. When you approach the holy table, you must be entirely full of love and light, having a God in your midst.

n. 377, to a nun, September 4, 1694

Jesus has come forth from the womb of His glorious Mother in order to be, through His own power, sown in the field of His Church, and the Church receives the power of the sower in the divine Eucharist; and it is through the adorable Eucharist that He sows Himself in our hearts. The holy Gospel says that the seed is the word of God, and the word of God is His Word and the Word was made flesh in order to come to dwell with us. It is by means of the Incarnation that He comes to us and by means of the Holy Eucharist that He is sown in our hearts. Therefore, it is Jesus Christ Himself who is this mysterious seed, and whom you should try to receive in the field of your heart.

n. 86, Conference on the Gospel, Luke 8:5–15

You will receive Communion today, please, with the dispositions in which the holy and loving Providence of God will place you...

Give yourself again entirely to Him and to His divine governance, content that God is satisfied in Himself and that He is satisfied with you as will please Him, without your senses taking any part in it. Remain in the state of being a victim which Jesus has in the Most Holy Sacrament, desiring to be immolated in His love. We will never be worthy of Communion, having no such power in ourselves; but Jesus Christ, through His part in Holy Communion, has sanctified ours and has merited for us the grace to receive Communion. Do not allow this favor which Jesus Christ granted you to be fruitless. Do not be surprised to feel nothing in your prayer; go forward without clinging to the anxiety which proceeds from your pride.

n. 3022, to the Countess of Châteauvieux

Let us always receive Communion very humbly, not for ourselves, but for God's glory, for the interests of His honor on earth, for the good of His Church and the souls who are His. We are members of Our Lord, of His holy Mother, and of all the saints;[1] in this capacity, we must do what they did and desired to do. We must do what they want us to do and what they would do and what they would think must be done for God's glory and for the good of His Church if they were on earth. It is necessary that we be theirs for Communion and that we receive Communion in their spirit, as if they lived in us and had the right to make use of us more than we do ourselves; we must think that we have no right to ourselves, being sinners. We must think that all that we are is forfeit to Jesus and to those who are His, and that we must be theirs for everything which they desire, renouncing our wills in order to live in theirs and our spirit to live from theirs. We should give ourselves to them so as to live in this manner.

Therefore, let us be detached from ourselves for this purpose and accustom ourselves to do it without trouble; let us do it with joy.

n. 2213, Essay on Holy Communion

---

[1] In French, *de tous les saints et saintes*: of all the saints, both male and female.

At the evening recreation, our worthy Mother spoke about the dispositions Holy Communion requires. "Receive Communion every day if you want," she said, "I desire it greatly, but I also desire that Holy Communion produce in you the death of yourself. Jesus Christ should make an impression of His states in a soul who receives Communion often.[2] They should be imprinted on the soul, and we should see them there in order to conform to His life; we should manifest them by our actions and words, and,

---

[2] In speaking of the "states" of Jesus, Mother Mectilde follows the school of Cardinal Bérulle. As Arthur Burton Calkins explains: "The exterior dimension of the mystery, which consists in the deeds that Christ performed, is past and unrepeatable, but the interior dimension, which is comprised of the dispositions and inward feelings that Christ had in each of His mysteries, is eternal. These interior dispositions of the soul of Christ are called in Bérullian language *states*. Whereas the exterior dimension of the mysteries of Christ is transitory, the interior dimension is eternal. Let us allow the great Cardinal to give us his own examples: 'The Infancy of the Son of God is but a transitory state, the circumstances are already past, He is a Child no longer; yet there is something Divine in this mystery, that still continues in Heaven, operating as then in a method of grace for souls on earth, whom it pleases Jesus Christ to move and consecrate to this lowly first state of His Person. We even see that Jesus has conceived the incorporation of a measure of His Passion in the state of His Glory, imprinting therein His Scars; so if He could thus preserve something of His Passion in His Glorious Body, wherefore should He not preserve something in His Soul of the consummated states of His Glory? Yet that which He retains of His Passion both in Body and Soul, is life and glory, and He suffers neither in Soul nor Body; and that which remains in Him of the mysteries that on earth form a means of grace is now applicable to souls chosen to receive it. Thus by these means of grace the mysteries of Jesus Christ, His Infancy, His Passion and the rest, continue and live upon the earth, to the end of Time'" ("The Union of the Hearts of Jesus and Mary in St. Francis de Sales and St. John Eudes," *Miles Immaculatae* 25 [1989]: 488–89; the internal quotation is from *Œuvres complètes de Bérulle* [Paris: Migne, 1856], 1052–53, cited in Henri Bremond, *A Literary History of Religious Thought in France*, III: *The Triumph of Mysticism*, trans. K. L. Montgomery [London: S.P.C.K., 1936], 59–60). For Bérulle, we can enter into these states in such a way that they are reproduced in ourselves.

when occasion arises, we must put into practice Jesus Christ's virtues...

"To receive Communion fruitfully, that adorable Sacrament must produce its effects in you. In fact, I am anxious when I see someone receiving Communion frequently and she does not take on the mind of Jesus Christ and has no resemblance to Him.

"I do not tell you not to receive Communion—understand my words properly—but I *do* say to you, in communicating often, to live according to the grace of the Communion, clothing yourself in Jesus Christ and asking for His spirit and living only for Him. And for this, it is necessary, I repeat to you, that you die to yourself."

n. 2108, Informal Conversations, May 3, 1694

Go to Communion to receive Jesus Christ my Master, but pray to Him that the strong will destroy the weak; no longer return to yourself. It is very surprising to me that we see in a soul other things than Jesus Christ after having received Him...

What happiness Holy Communion is! I cannot get over it, and I am surprised that after so many Holy Communions one sees in us anything other than Jesus Christ. "*Misit me vivens Pater*: as I live for the Father, in the same way those who eat Me will live from Me and for Me."[3] These words are adorable. How they contain such mysteries! Oh! If Our Lord granted me the mercy to live only for Him, you know very well that I would not be in a hurry to go to paradise! I would gladly offer God to live nine hundred years if such were His good pleasure! And why? Because I would have paradise itself in me, because Jesus, being my life, the Three Divine Persons, who are inseparable, would be in my soul as in heaven, and, through Jesus, the source of my life, they would

---

[3] Cf. Jn 6:58 [57]: As the living Father hath sent me, and I live by the Father; so he that eateth me, the same also shall live by me.

receive in me adoration and love worthy of Them, which is the only reason we desire paradise...

All that the soul has to do in approaching Holy Communion is to ennothing and humble herself, so that Jesus alone appears in the sight of God His Father, who can only delight in His Son, and then she can say to Him boldly, "*Respice, Domine, in faciem Christi tui*. O Lord, look upon the face of your Christ."[4]

O ineffable and adorable mystery of Holy Communion! This is the banquet which is spoken of in the Gospel today, where the master of the feast says, "My friend, come up higher."[5] For God, seeing the soul profoundly ennothinged at the nearness of Holy Communion out of reverence for this divine majesty, is charmed by its humility. He says to him in the depth of his soul, "Come up higher." In reality, it is to make him go up as high as dwelling in God and to transform him totally into Himself, and that is a dogma of faith. I know a person who saw a soul coming from Communion who had become totally Jesus Christ. That is: Jesus Christ alone appeared in all of him, even in his outward appearance. This is confirmed by the words of Jesus Christ, *Misit me vivens Pater*, etc.,[6] and by the testimony of the holy Fathers who say that, through Holy Communion, the soul is united to Christ in the most perfect union, that the soul becomes bone of His bones, flesh of His flesh![7] Oh! How astonishing this is! And this union lasts not only as long as the sacred species endures, but always, if the soul remains in a state of grace—not that Jesus Christ is sacramentally present, but He remains in the soul in a mystical and spiritual way. He is there as the principle of life.

n. 20, Conference on Holy Communion

---

[4] Ps 83:10 [84:9].

[5] Lk 14:10. Lk 14:1–11 is read on the Sixteenth Sunday after Pentecost.

[6] Cf. Jn 6:58[57].

[7] Cf. Gen 2:23.

The Life of Jesus in Us

B E COMPLETELY FILLED with the fullness of Jesus Christ, and I desire that the work He did in the soul of Zaccheus, by His divine gaze, have the same effect on you today. This is the subject of the Gospel of the Dedication [of a Church].[1] Your soul is the temple consecrated by the three divine Persons of the Most Holy Trinity. It is the house of Jesus Christ. But remember that He said in speaking about it, *Domus mea domus orationis vocabitur*, My house shall be called a house of prayer. At Holy Communion renew the dedication of your soul, desiring to belong perfectly to Jesus.

n. 2754, Conference for the feast of the Dedication of a Church

My Sisters, what happiness we have in Jesus Christ and through Jesus Christ, who is given to us by the holy Mother of God! Yes, we receive Him really and truly, each one in particular through Holy Communion, and we must receive this infinite gift from the hands and heart of the most holy Virgin each time that we have the joy of receiving Communion. We must have love and gratitude towards that Mother of mercy. But above all, we should make a faithful "use" of Jesus Christ, who is completely ours—not only as long as the sacred species subsists in us, for even when Jesus Christ is no longer sacramentally present, He remains in the soul always spiritually through His divine spirit, His grace, and His virtues.

---

[1] Namely, Lk 19:1–10.

St. Ignatius [of Antioch], the martyr whose feast we celebrate today, is for us a faithful witness. This great saint so loved Jesus Christ that in the midst of his torments, he longed only for the love of Jesus, speaking only of Jesus and rejoicing that the teeth of the leopards and lions were tearing his body, in order, as he said, to be the wheat of Jesus. My Sisters, we should be animated with the same zeal and the same love that this great saint had for Jesus Christ. And since, through Holy Communion, He feeds us with His own substance, He also asks that we feed Him if we want Him to live in us, for although He is life by His very essence, He is in us only insofar as we will give Him food that is worthy of Him…

Mortification will be the mill to break and crush our passions, our bad habits, and to destroy everything in us that might be displeasing in His eyes.

n. 323, Conference for the vigil of the Purification, 1664

Oh! What marvelous things Jesus intends to do in the souls whom He has chosen as His children. One of the most miraculous, my Sisters, is to make us live from His Eucharistic life. What is this life? Jesus Christ is in the Eucharist to be eaten by us, to nourish us, to sustain us with Himself, and His intention is to satisfy Himself with us for His delight.

How can He nourish Himself? My Sisters, by eating Him, He consumes us, and, being in our hearts, we are within His Heart. He lives in us according to the life we give Him. Just as we put Him to death by sin, in the same way, we give Him life by our fidelity. We see by experience that, according to the different states and dispositions of souls, He lives wonderfully in some persons and languishes in others. Accordingly, our care and vigilance, our love and faithfulness, give Him life more or less powerfully. Therefore, my Sisters, is it in our power to make Jesus live in us? Yes, by His grace.

Oh! Far too greedy is the soul to whom Jesus in the holy

Eucharist is not enough...[2] Let us eat, my Sisters, this adorable Bread, but after having been filled with it, let us no longer ask for the flesh pots of Egypt; this is a Bread that contains life in itself. The one who eats only to sustain life does not seek the pleasure of taste when eating... Taste it with a pure and naked faith, and you will see that it has the taste of the living God; eating it in this way, you will have life in you.

n. 2562, Essay

I have not had time to write a word about the holy Gospel[3] as you wanted, but I will tell you only this: that your soul should adore the great Prophet who was raised up from the midst of the earth to visit His people. Here is this adorable Prophet in the august Eucharist, who leaves the tabernacle to visit your soul, which is His elect and the chosen one of His Heart. He comes to do in you what He did in the past to the son of the widow in the Gospel, whom He brought back to life.

Your soul is dead if it is not animated by the life of Jesus. He comes in this Sacrament of love in order to communicate it to you. Be like the dead man in his coffin: without any resistance to the divine power. Allow Jesus to touch you and say to you today, *Surge a mortuis*. Rise from the death of sin and of yourself. Rise from the midst of the dead, and Jesus Christ will enlighten you.[4]

However, a resurrected soul is the kind that can no longer see anything but Jesus: to that soul He is life and light. This is what you receive in Holy Communion. Being thus resurrected, He gives you to your mother, the holy Church, who receives you

---

[2] See note 5 on the following page.

[3] Lk 7:11–16, read on the Fifteenth Sunday after Pentecost.

[4] Cf. Eph 5:14. Rise thou that sleepest, and arise from the dead: and Christ shall enlighten thee.

with marvelous joy, inasmuch as she sees that Jesus has enlivened you with His life of grace, of love, and of holiness. Oh! What consolation the Church has, and how great is her jubilation, when she receives such children!

n. 2106, *to the Countess of Châteauvieux,* 1662

I am surprised that after having received my God—all that He is in Himself—so many times, we ask for something more. What more do you want? In giving Himself to you, He gives you everything without any reservation. By receiving Him in Holy Communion, you receive the Father and the Holy Spirit, that is *de fide.* You receive His power and all His divine perfections. Ah! Do not ask for anything else! "Too greedy is the one," says a great soul, "for whom God is not enough."[5]

n. 3140, *Conference for the Feast of Corpus Christi*

Ah! What an astonishing thing that after Communion we are not on fire, and that I myself am all ice after so many Communions. One saint (Mary of Egypt) was completely on fire after a single Communion. Yes, a single Communion is enough to make us burn all our life and to have this fire always with us. Do you think that, being no longer in choir, and being in your rooms, or elsewhere, this fire is no longer with you and that it does not see us anymore? Oh! You are mistaken, my Sisters; it sees you always and is with you everywhere.

In the past, God stood at the gate of the Temple in Jerusalem and cried out, "Whoever is thirsty, let him come to Me that he

---

[5] Mother Mectilde alludes to the saying of St. Augustine: "Quid avarius illo cui Deo sufficere non potuit?" (*Homilies on the First Epistle of John*, tract. 8, par. 6 [SC 75:350]; cf. *Sermon* 255), which is also cited by Meister Eckhart in his *Book of Divine Consolation* and by Madame Acarie, who took it from St. Teresa of Jesus (cf. Bremond, *Histoire Littéraire*, 2:203–9). Mother Mectilde adapts it in accord with her own charism.

may drink."[6] And during this octave,[7] Our Lord comes to the door of the Tabernacle, where He is exposed before our eyes, in order to cry out to us and say to us, "Whoever wants fire, let him come to Me!" Ah! In how many thousands of churches will He be alone! Have the intention to adore Him in all the churches where He will be exposed. Be very silent; all of the holy Fathers say that one cannot be a truly interior person and a great talker.[8] Therefore, be very faithful about keeping silence...

Oh! This God of Fire, He has too many graces for Himself, He wants to fill us with them! Ah! If I myself had this fire, I would help you to burn with it by telling you about the graces that people will not want during this octave, and even in our Church... Go present yourselves to Our Lord to receive them; ask Him for them, and pray that He will give you all the ones that others will not want.

n. 8, Conference for the Feast of Corpus Christi

Through Holy Communion Jesus enters into us to continue in each soul His holy life, to continue in each of us His adoration, His prayer, His love, and His sacrifice, in such a way that, when we have received Communion, we should not do anything at all except cling to Him, and unite or allow our heart and our mind to be united to all the actions that He brings about in us, working in us in our name, that is, for us, as if we were the ones doing it.

He comes to us to be our life and our action, and since we do not know how to pray, or adore, or sacrifice as is necessary—in a

---

[6] Jn 7:37.

[7] From the time of its widespread observance in the 14th century until 1955, the feast of Corpus Christi enjoyed an octave. So firmly established was this octave that when Jesus appeared to St. Margaret Mary Alacoque on June 16, 1675, He requested that a feast of His Sacred Heart be instituted on "the Friday after the octave of Corpus Christi."

[8] Cf. Ps 139:12 [140:11].

manner worthy of His greatness and the dignity of God—Jesus does all this in us after Holy Communion and continues for as long as the soul is submissive to the movements of His inspirations and ceases her own activity, in order to give herself exclusively to the operation of Jesus in her, by a simple gaze of faith and loving acquiescence.

n. 1539, Essay

If you cannot communicate sacramentally, communicate by desire and love. In this way, unite yourself to and be transformed into Jesus in the Most Holy Eucharist, and to His good pleasure secretly at work in you. Be faithful about receiving everything from His hand and do not be troubled about anything.

n. 2290, to a nun, rue St. Louis, Paris

Let us look, my Sisters, let us look at Jesus Christ as the Way we should follow, as the Truth we should believe, and as the Life with which our souls should be animated, since it is this divine life that He gives us as food, like the good shepherd, in the Most Holy Eucharist...

Having received Jesus in Holy Communion, we should feed our souls with His grace and His virtues, which we possess in Him, that is, "use" Jesus Christ. Is an occasion presented to practice humility, patience, gentleness? Do we draw on the grace and power in Jesus Christ? Let us consider that indeed He practiced these virtues, and let us conform to His example. This is what nourishes our soul, which will live from Jesus Christ, or rather, Jesus Christ will live in it in an ineffable manner...

Oh my Sisters, what happiness to know Jesus Christ! This knowledge is not acquired by the elevation of our own thoughts, which certain souls use like wings to fly to God, believing they can reach Him by force of speed. No, no, we must, like little birds, small and weak, remain in the nest of our nothingness, and there grow strong and believe in the grace of divine love, which will warm our heart and strengthen its wings to take its flight toward God.

n. 1523, Conference on the Gospel of the Good Shepherd

Continue your practices and Holy Communion: it will help you to go out of yourself in no small measure; I find nothing more efficacious. There are souls who receive much from Jesus through Holy Communion. It is also through this precious means that He changes the soul into Himself and imprints on it His divine likeness. Communion is a mystery for souls.

n. 3121, to the Countess of Rochefort, Thursday after Easter

The intention we must have in Holy Communion is to give ourselves to God and for Him to possess us absolutely, doing in us all that He desires to do; and then, let us leave ourselves wholly surrendered to Him, agreeing and consenting to all that He will do with us in time and in eternity.

n. 576, Essay

My very dear lady, I beseech you to be completely Jesus Christ's, just as Jesus Christ is completely yours in the Host... Separate yourself from all that can distract you in the slightest from His pure love, and remain in this spirit of victimhood, since in reality you are a victim with Jesus Christ. You form part of Him. Lose yourself entirely in Him, and be very faithful in seeing and receiving everything in the order of His love. Be content with His most holy will, and pray that in mercy He will protect me and bring about my conversion.

Let us be again completely Jesus Christ's, with a new love and a new fidelity, for we are His in a way that is, in a certain manner, new to us. This is why we ought to be completely renewed in Him and by Him in the Most Holy Sacrament and begin to lead a life that has some resemblance to His divine life, hidden and ennothinged in the Most Holy Eucharist...

n. 167, to the Countess of Châteauvieux

The eternal Father is the *paterfamilias* who made the great banquet, described in the Gospel, where He gives us His own Son.[9] Oh! Who can see all the operations that God brings about in all the souls after Holy Communion! The effects are as diverse as each soul who receives Communion. They always tend toward ennothingment. How many times have you seen your plans and your desires brought to nothing in Holy Communion—sometimes even your own acts? At the time of Communion, have you not felt some devotion and as soon as you have communicated, you are totally poor, stripped, and without power to do anything? This is because Our Lord draws you into His poverty and nakedness, so that He may be everything in you and that you may be nothing. Allow yourself to be destroyed, and allow Our Lord to be master in you, and may He reign supreme in you.

In Holy Communion, He draws us into Himself and He passes into us; He is our thanksgiving, our love… We say again, hardly touching on the matter, that in Holy Communion we have gratitude, acts of thanksgiving, and love worthy of God Himself, since it is He Himself who does all of this in us, for us. As for us, let us try to mix nothing of our own into it by our own working, but let us allow Him to act alone; let us remain at His feet in tranquility.

n. 2017, Essay on Holy Communion

It is the intention of Jesus Christ Our Lord in the Most Holy Sacrament of the Altar to make you live with His life. He desires it, and I dare to say He begs it of you, having an infinite desire that the souls in this house be the object of His delight.

We must unite ourselves to Our Lord Jesus Christ in our divine Sacrament, asking for a share in His divine dispositions, living from His life as members of this adorable Head—and this

---

[9] Lk 14:16–24, read on the Second Sunday after Pentecost; cf. Mt 22:2–14; Mt 25:1–13.

must be the effect of our daily Communions. It is the obligation of all Catholics.

n. 337, Chapter for a new house[10]

After Holy Communion, remain in silence, in faith, in reverence, and in love, above your senses. Do not be surprised to feel nothing, to be able to say nothing, to be unable to think of many beautiful things. You do not receive Communion to find life in yourself, but to find death. Therefore, leave yourself in death, so that God may give you life through Himself. Remain in a loving acquiescence toward all that God does in you and all that He desires of you, continuing your precious abandonment in your sacrifice. In this way you will do what God desires and will not be working against His operation... It is not enough to bring this disposition to Communion, or even to have it after Communion; it should continue in you always, so that you may always be in the state of abandonment.

n. 530, to the Countess of Châteauvieux

After Holy Communion, remain in silence as much as you can, and allow Jesus Christ to be your adorer towards His Father and to supply[11] for you in everything. Say only, *Amen*... Leave the rest to divine Providence, which will take care of it.

n. 2528, to a nun, rue Cassette

Oh Holy Communion, divine and ineffable, which unites us to Jesus Christ and makes us pass into Him! Let us remain there, humbled; let us be lost in Jesus Christ! May we no longer see ourselves or any of the things of earth! Oh! If we were truly

---

[10] The term "chapter" here refers to a talk given by the Superior to the community, typically after the Office of Prime.

[11] The phrase could also be rendered "supplement, make up the difference."

attentive to this great mystery, we would not amuse ourselves with so many useless things which fill our minds and hearts and empty them of God. Let us leave behind these things in order to abide in Jesus Christ, and let us apply ourselves only to loving and adoring Him. When we are attached to Him in this way, He will take care of all the rest...

Today is the feast of the Dedication.[12] I like dedications: they remind me that our souls are consecrated to God through baptism, and every time we receive Communion, Jesus Christ comes to renew this consecration, and we must do it with Him.

n. 513, Conference

Our Lord comes into us through Holy Communion; He is incarnate anew, so to speak, in all who receive Him, so that we may keep and manifest Him by our good works and express His virtues in the course of our life. There are infinite mysteries in Holy Communion, my Sisters, since when you possess Jesus Christ in your bosom, Jesus Christ possesses you. But you do not change Him into yourself, rather He changes you into Himself, and, presenting you to His Father like this, reclothed with Himself, we can only be very pleasing to Him.

He also performs His office of High Priest by means of Holy Communion: the heart of the person who receives Him is the altar, and on it He sacrifices all that is opposed to Him.[13] There-

---

[12] That is, the dedication of a church.

[13] "What Christ wants first of all is that His sacrifice—the unique source of salvation for the world—should remain present throughout the world's history, to carry it in His grace. If He Himself is present to us, it is in the act of this sacrifice, of which he is both priest and victim. Therefore, His presence in the Eucharist is a supremely *active* presence: He is present there as bearing the whole of history in the unique grace of His redemptive sacrifice. He is present there as building up the Church, which is His body, in the power of His resurrected body. He is present to His Church and through her to the world, as accomplishing in and through her His work of salvation. . . . We have emphasized the link between the Eucharist and the Incarnation. What is

fore, my Sisters, we have only to unite ourselves to Our Lord in this precious time, gently acquiescing to what He does in us, without being encumbered by many multiplied acts, since all that we can do of ourselves is nothing compared to what Our Lord Himself does in us.

Ask the most holy Virgin to prepare you to celebrate this great feast, so that you can receive the effects of her dear Son's birth. Entreat her to bring it about spiritually in you. Remain at her feet, unite yourself to her, and ask for a share of her faith, her profound humility—but, first of all, for the desires and holy ardor she had seeing her divine Son born into the world.

n. 1591, Conference on the Nativity of the Lord

My Sisters, do you truly understand what one Communion is? What! A God who gives Himself absolutely to you, that is, all that He is and all that He has in Himself! He comes in order to draw you to Himself completely, to change you into Himself and make you entirely one with Him. Only one Communion would be necessary to make a soul go out of herself and pass into Jesus Christ, because, I repeat, He does not come to you except to draw you into Himself. Yes, my Sisters, Our Lord comes to us to take possession of our hearts and make them pass into His adorable Heart. Ask Him to attract you to Himself, to hide you in Himself... that you may dwell in Him completely hidden and completely lost, in such a way that you are no longer anything

---

at stake for our faith in the affirmation of the Real Presence of Christ in the Eucharist is the *fullness* of the mystery of the Incarnation: the role of Christ's humanity in the plan of salvation, in the work of the world's redemption. . . . The Incarnation is not God's coming to live on earth for a few years. It is God's definitive engagement with our history. Christ dwells with us, under the sign which He Himself has given us, and which is His Church. At the heart of the Church's life is the Eucharist, which is, in a unique and incomparable way, the mystery of Christ's presence among us" (Dom Georges Lefebvre, *Dieu présent*).

and that He alone is everything. Ask Him to rule absolutely in you, to be the source of all your thoughts, your words, your actions—in short, that everything you do be only the fruit of His own Spirit, becoming perfectly united with Him. Oh! My Sisters, what I would have to say to you about the mysteries worked in souls through Holy Communion! I could discuss it with you for whole hours, if I had more facility in speaking. Yes, I would say wondrous things; I would do it with all my heart, if I had the ability. But the strength is lacking to me; I must be silent in spite of myself.

n. 2460, Informal Conversations, March 19, 1694

To Become
Another Jesus Christ

I THINK YOU ARE ALL renewed in the desire to live a new life.
Please God, my Sisters, that this little saying from the Apocalypse may apply to you and to me: *Ecce nova facio omnia,*[1]
that we are new creatures and that we walk in newness of life as
St. Paul exhorts us...[2]

It is true, and St. John says it out of awe, that "God so loved the
world that He gave His Son for it..."[3] The Father gives Him to us
in the Incarnation for the salvation of all men, but the love of the
Son does not stop there. He is not satisfied to have borne all the
rigor of divine justice and suffered such an ignominious death by
being made the victim for sinners; I believe that He continues to
endure these humiliations in our Most Holy Sacrament...

Are these not the excesses of Jesus's love, which found this
invention to attract into our souls the holiness of God, who had
nothing in common with His creatures? But Jesus, by the transformation of the soul in itself that He brings about through Holy
Communion, attracts the gaze of the whole august Trinity, which
is joined to the soul in an ineffable manner.

n. 1692, *Conference for the day after New Year's Day,* 1663

We must not only have charity for our Sisters, but embrace
everyone in this union of the charity of Jesus Christ. Isn't this

[1] Rev 21:5. Behold, I make all things new.
[2] Rm 6:4.
[3] Cf. Jn 3:16.

what He wishes through Holy Communion, which we receive so often; and how can it be, after so many Communions, that we have any other inclination than that of Jesus Christ, who is all charity, gentleness, and patience in this divine Sacrament? Oh! It is certain that if we prepare ourselves by charity itself to receive Him, He would communicate to us all His loving dispositions...

We must die if we desire to enter into the dispositions of Jesus Christ in this divine Sacrament and become another Jesus Christ. That is what He wishes. And who would conceive the happiness of a soul thus become Jesus Christ? It is beyond words; the soul has the liberty of the children of God.[4] You will say to me, "You speak of a joy and a divine liberty, but at the same time it is always necessary to renounce oneself and to die unceasingly?" Yes, my Sisters, the one is arrived at only through the other. The beginnings of it are difficult; one finds bitterness there, but the progress is sweet.

n. 217, Chapter on the excellence of charity

My dear Sisters, the Gospel for today[5] shows us the Transfiguration of Our Lord Jesus Christ, who appeared on Mount Tabor absolutely blazing with glory and majesty, with a beauty and a splendor wholly divine. This was a beauty that had been conferred on His most holy humanity from the moment of His incarnation by the hypostatic union with the Word, and hence, was natural to Him. But His love kept it hidden until that time by a miracle of His omnipotence, so as to make Him like us [in condition]. Hence, He caused a cessation of the miracle, in order to show to His beloved disciples in those blessed moments a sample of His beatific glory...

Jesus Christ will cause a real transfiguration in us. My Sisters, this is the effect of a good Communion: to transform the whole

[4] Cf. Rm 8:21.
[5] Mt 17:1–9.

soul into God...[6] Holy Communion, as I have said to you in the past, transforms the entire soul into Jesus Christ (supposing that the soul receives in a state of grace). This is a truth of the faith, maintained and preached by the Fathers of the Church, because at that time, the soul is entirely luminous, although it perceives nothing of the sort, and although the soul is in a condition of darkness and privation. In those blessed moments (that is, as long as the sacred species endures), the soul is in possession of all paradise. It becomes another Jesus Christ by the most intimate union...

Remain in possession of this transfiguration which He has made today of your souls in Him through Holy Communion. Keep it carefully by the practice of the virtues of Jesus, which will put you in possession of the second transfiguration, that of perfection in God. This is the grace which holy Church offers to all her children on this holy day of the Transfiguration of Jesus. Pray to Him to give me a small share. Go in peace.

n. 2111, *Conference for the Transfiguration of the Lord, August* 1663

I have told you before that it is a dogma of faith to believe that after Holy Communion, as long as the species subsists in the person, the soul is completely transformed in Jesus Christ, and if the soul were visible, one could see only Jesus Christ in her. (I assume it is in a state of grace.) But after we have consumed the holy and adorable species, the reason this transformation does not continue in us—a transformation which is the intention of Jesus Christ—comes from the fact that after our thanksgiving we

---

[6] United to Jesus through faith and love, the communicant "is transformed into him and becomes his member," says St. Thomas Aquinas, "for this food is not changed into the one who eats it, but turns into itself the one who takes it. . . . This is a food capable of making man divine and inebriating him with divinity" (*Commentary on John*, ch. 6, lec. 7). Cf. *Summa theologiae* III, q. 73, a. 3, ad 2.

are too easily dissipated, we fill ourselves with creatures, and then we return to ourselves, namely, to our moods and habits. We are not faithful to the practice of mortification, and this is the reason there is so little fruit from so many Communions which I call unworthy (for those made in mortal sin are sacrilegious). Yes, they are unworthy of the holiness and love of Jesus Christ, lodging Him in a heart impure and defiled with a thousand faults that we take no trouble to correct. We should never approach Holy Communion except with the resolution to mortify one passion or another, an inclination, or some attachment that we know to be displeasing to God—the fruit of one good Communion being a fidelity to the practice of mortification.

And I have no doubt that Our Lord would transform into Himself a soul who would be faithful to this practice: that is His intention and His heart's desire. I do not say that at first it would have complete perfection; no, that is for some chosen souls; those are extraordinary graces. You will observe that, just as there are diverse states in Jesus Christ, and infinite virtues and perfections in Him, there are always various transformations to be made in a soul during the whole course of its life, no matter how advanced it may be. This is done by degrees, according to His good pleasure. If a soul is very faithful and puts up no obstacles to God's designs, it will soon be completely transformed into Him. Just as there are various degrees of union in the interior life, so there are various states and various stages of transformation which Jesus causes in souls.

In Holy Communion, I observe two different ways of praying. The first is that of souls united to Jesus Christ, through whom they are always at prayer. Having heart and soul united to God, they have no great trouble: it is Jesus Christ who prays in them. The other way of prayer is that of souls who tend toward this union and who unite themselves to Jesus Christ by loving desire, and who in prayer unite themselves to His divine understanding, and to the affections and desires of His divine will. This done, they remain in silence and reverence at His feet, clinging to Jesus, without whom they can do nothing. He says it Himself in the holy Gospel: "Without Me you can do nothing. No one can go to the Father except through Me. If you are not united to me as the branch to the vine, you will bear no fruit."[7] And a great many other passages indicate to us our need to be united to Jesus Christ. He also says, "I am the way, the truth, and the life."[8] In these three words are contained all the perfection and holiness of Christians. Prayer that is not made *in* Jesus Christ and *through* Jesus Christ is ineffectual and cannot be accepted by God.

n. 1659, Conference on Holy Communion

Jesus Christ instituted this divine Sacrament in order to give glory to His Father and to come to us to change us into Himself...

You are fed with Jesus Christ, Sisters; are you another Jesus Christ?

Since the time you received Communion, we should see only Jesus Christ. If someone asked you if your actions are the actions of Jesus Christ, your words the words of Jesus Christ, your thoughts the thoughts of Jesus Christ—if you were asked to imitate God in His divinity, you would have some excuse, saying that He is elevated in His divine perfections, and that this is beyond you: His power, His immensity, and the rest. But one is offering you Jesus Christ in His holy humanity, having been subject to the same weaknesses as you, yet without sin.[9] His love made Him institute our divine Sacrament so that, consuming Him, you would receive His power, and so that you might be totally His. It is not with this mystery as with some others, my Sisters, for those pass, granting the grace attached to the mys-

---

[7] Cf. Jn 14:6, 15:5.
[8] Jn 14:6.
[9] Cf. Heb 4:15.

tery when they are presented to us by the Church.[10] Our great mystery endures always, it does not pass like the others; He is always ready to give you the proofs of His love, today, tomorrow, every day...

Oh, my Sisters, a soul who gives Him *carte blanche*, that is, who puts no limit on the powers of Jesus Christ or His designs, experiences miracles of grace! We must keep nothing back: Jesus Christ gives Himself entirely to you, so why would you not give yourself entirely to Him?...

Pray to the most holy Virgin to quicken your hearts. You should never receive Communion unless you have called on her and asked her to prepare your heart that it may be worthy to receive her Son—or rather, ask her that she give you her own.

n. 3142, Chapter for the Feast of Corpus Christi

My Sisters, what did you do today? You all received Communion. Our Lord says in the Gospel that the one who eats His Flesh

[10] Special graces are given throughout the liturgical year, in accordance with the various mysteries recounted and re-presented in particular feasts and commemorations; but the grace of communion with Christ in the Eucharist remains constant. As Mother Mectilde teaches: "God renews His graces and mercies in the great feasts. That is why, although the mysteries are not taking place any longer, Our Lord does not cease to renew and produce in our souls the grace of each mystery, in Holy Communion" (n. 3157, *Conférences et chapitres de notre mère Mectilde*, ed. Bayeux [1985], 101). Dom Prosper Guéranger comments: "The celebration of those mysteries [in the Church calendar] was not an empty pageant, acted for the sake of being looked at. Each one of them brought with it a special grace, which produced in our souls the reality signified by the rites of the liturgy. At Christmas Christ was born within us; at Passiontide He passed on and into us His sufferings and atonements; at Easter He communicated to us His glorious, His untrammeled life; in His Ascension he drew us after Him, and this even to heaven's summit; in a word, as the apostle expresses all this working, 'Christ was formed in us' (Gal 4:19)" (*The Liturgical Year*, vol. 10: Time after Pentecost, book I, trans. Dom Laurence Shepherd [Great Falls, MT: St. Bonaventure Publications, 2000], 3). Cf. below, 81–82.

and drinks His Blood abides in Him,[11] and in another place He says, "My Father and I will come to him and we will make our abode with him."[12] Therefore, we are all divinized by His coming to us. At that time, He causes a transformation: not that God is transformed into us, but that we are transformed into God.

Perhaps a Sister will say to me that we do not experience this, that we always feel a certain weight from our passions, the same weaknesses, the same moods. It must amaze and embarrass us to see how little fruit we obtain from so holy an action, which is the noblest, the greatest, the most important in Christianity. If we truly understood this mystery of God with us, we would have such joy in receiving it and at the same time a reverence so profound that it would give us . . . fear in approaching it.

O blessed possession of God, how you should be cherished! How happy is the soul who knows how to keep Him and make Him live in her!

n. 2614, Conference for the feast of St. Ursula

Oh! My Sisters, this is the mystery of mysteries for us. Jesus Christ enters the soul in Holy Communion. . . He passes into this holy sanctuary in the most intimate part of our souls, where He renews His adorable mysteries, principally that of His sacrifice, in a way most profitable to the soul. For, Jesus being substantially united to us by the Eucharist, we become (according to the opinion of the Fathers) simply one with Him; for we are bone of His bones, flesh of His flesh, and so fully united to Him that this union fills the whole Church with astonishment; she cannot admire it enough. This is a dogma of faith and we must believe it.

But I ask you, when you receive Communion, is it you who cause that union and transformation? Certainly not; it is Jesus, by virtue of His divine Sacrament. It is enough on your part that

[11] Jn 6:56.
[12] Jn 14:23.

you are in a state of grace, and all the rest is done by Jesus Christ's infinite love. This being so, and a dogma of faith, why is it that we teach souls nothing about how to conduct themselves and what they should do during this divine exchange? I say that they need do very little: only two things. First, they should adhere to Jesus in the depth of their wills, and second, they should not interfere by attempting to know, to enter, and to perceive what is happening in them, to feel it and be assured of it.

It is necessary to remain recollected, if the soul can, and simply give its consent to all that is happening in it through the divine and personal reality of Jesus Christ. If the Sisters cannot remain peaceful, or have neither reverence nor concentration, let them say with all their hearts, along with the whole Church: *Amen*.

n. 610, Essay

What is the spirit of Jesus Christ in the Holy Eucharist? See if it is not a spirit of love and charity. Can we find or see a love greater than that of Him who gives Himself entirely to us, without holding anything back? And after this, will we not be all love and charity for our Sisters, being the daughters of a God whose charity reaches to infinity? This is the great charity you should have for each other. It is by this that you will be known as my disciples, says Our Lord.[13]

It is the proper effect of the Holy Eucharist to make us into Jesus Christ; and, in like manner, if we were able to see a soul when she comes from Communion, we could see nothing then except Jesus Christ.

How does it happen, then, that we do not remain in Him? One Communion should create a perfect transformation in us, and it should do so at the very moment of Communion. So why is it that we are always ourselves, proud, full of self-love, and

[13] Cf. Jn 13:35.

further, quick to follow our passions and indulge our senses? It is because we do not understand the greatness of this action; we do not have faith.

"But," you will say to me, "can these faults take away from us the graces of Holy Communion?" No, since its proper effect is to transform us, we cannot hinder that . . . but to live in imperfection in such a manner deprives us of the graces that Jesus Christ would have brought us in Holy Communion.

Do not cause such a great grace as this to be in vain, for is there anything greater than to be transformed into Jesus Christ? We do not cause this transformation; it is Jesus Christ Himself who causes it and who transforms us into Himself through this adorable Sacrament. He hides us in Himself, He absorbs us into Himself, His love carries us even to the point of uniting us to Him, in such a manner that we are simply one with Him. Can there be anything greater? Has Our Lord not extended His love even to excess? Ah! If we had the faith to believe it, and if we would think about how we receive a God of infinite majesty as He truly is, would we not be overwhelmed with reverence?

Let us try to approach Holy Communion with the most faith, reverence, and attention possible for us, so that, having these dispositions which Our Lord requires, He can freely work His divine effects in our soul. And let us make use of it as we should, my Sisters, for what a reckoning we shall have to give to God! I tell you, it is one of the greatest we will have at death—this one of such a great grace neglected, and which, nevertheless, we receive so often and with so little fruit. This should make us lament. After Holy Communion, does Jesus Christ live in us as He should live? Do we live from Him? Are we animated with His spirit? Do we practice His virtues? Alas! Far from it. How does this happen, since He does not keep anything to Himself? It is because we fail, as I said before, to make use of the grace of transformation that He works in us through this precious mystery.

Can Jesus Christ give us more than Himself? And since in Holy Communion He gives Himself completely to us—all that He is, and all that He has of what is great and holy, His virtues, His merits, and the rest of His adorable perfections—what more do you want? If Jesus Christ gave you some favor, some lights or ecstasies or raptures in prayer, these would be real graces; but what are they, compared to Jesus Christ? And besides, you would have cause for fear, since such things are subject to illusion, and we can be deceived. But regarding Holy Communion, there is nothing to be apprehensive about, since it is Our Lord in His own person who gives the reality of Himself. We are obliged to believe this.

Therefore, endeavor that Holy Communion may bring about in your souls a true transformation from now on; that you may no longer be seen, but Jesus Christ wholly in you; and also that you no longer see anything but Him in everything and everywhere—so that you may be like the Apostles, who saw Him truly in the mystery of His Transfiguration, and having come back to themselves, saw no longer either Moses or Elijah, or anything else: Jesus Christ alone was visible to their eyes.[14] That is where we must remain. May this divine object hold our sight and our attention; may we think only of Him, may we act only for Him, seek only Him.

Let us pray to the most holy Mother of God to prepare us for Holy Communion and to put us into a state to receive efficaciously the grace of transformation which Jesus Christ causes in us, so that, this grace remaining always at work, we may all blessedly abide in Jesus Christ. This is what I desire for you.

n. 3004, *Chapter on the Rule of St. Benedict* (*ch.* 74), *August* 1664

---

[14] Cf. Mt 17:8. And they lifting up their eyes saw no one but only Jesus.

Liturgy

THE MYSTERY OF the Incarnation is a mystery of love, and Holy Communion is its completion and consummation...

It is the glory of the eternal Father to see His Son humbled out of His love for Him, and to render to Him what we cannot because of our indigence. We have nothing except from Him and through Him; we must therefore receive Communion, but, as much as possible, in amazement at the excess of the mercies of Jesus, who renews in us the ineffable mystery of the Incarnation...

I said that Jesus enters into us through Holy Communion. He was there captive, in darkness, and in a kind of powerlessness. This is true, you know it, but this is not something to be troubled about, since it is what we are because of original sin. Therefore, this should not discourage us and make us sad, but rather delight us with amazement and oblige us to be more faithful to Him, as much as possible, through solitude and abandonment to His will, through silence and a continual gaze toward His goodness and His love.

n. 122, *to a nun, rue Cassette*

Here are the great mysteries that happened and with which we should still be filled: the institution of the Most Holy Eucharist, the death and resurrection of Our Lord, and our being united through them to the Incarnation. Let us see if we have participated in these great mysteries. If we have died with Jesus Christ, we will rise with Him.[1] There is no mystery which does not

---

[1] 2 Tim 2:11.

bring its graces; but all of them are contained in the august Sacrament of the Altar, and every time we receive Communion, Jesus comes to us in order to renew them and to give us a share in His glorious resurrection; for the mysteries of Our Lord are only given to us that we may share in their graces and that they may produce their effects in us and the graces they contain, and make us live a life conformed to that of Our Lord...[2]

For if we are with Him, and if we are the companions of His sufferings, we will also be companions in His glory.[3]

n. 2949, Conference after Easter, 1694

When one awaits a great gift, one thinks about it at night as well as during the day. We await the birth of Jesus in our hearts, which is the gift of gifts. You desire it ardently, and you have already done so millions of times, but these were ineffectual and passing desires. The holy Virgin desired to give Him to the world, the holy Patriarchs desired Him, and we see that the Divine Office is all desires. Let us ask the holy Virgin, Mother of God, to show us the preparations necessary for us, so that her Son may be born into our souls...

The eternal Father gives us Jesus every day in Holy Communion. He "so loved the world that He gave His only Son."[4] Oh! The excellence of that gift, the gift of gifts! It surpasses our understanding...

It is faith that gives us entry into the mysteries; without faith we will not be admitted. There are two kinds of faith: a speculative and a practical faith. Speculative faith without practical faith

[2] Mother Mectilde draws upon a rich tradition of meditation on how we participate in the "mysteries of Jesus" through the liturgy, the Mass, and the Blessed Sacrament. For a thorough presentation, see John Saward, *Cradle of Redeeming Love: The Theology of the Christmas Mystery* (San Francisco: Ignatius Press, 2002), 47–120.

[3] Cf. Rm 8:17.

[4] Jn 3:16.

will not save us. To believe that God is in the Most Holy Eucharist is a totally divine faith, which causes us to see and understand a God who is poor, humble, ennothinged, reduced as if to a speck to come to us and to be eaten by us. What great mysteries faith discloses to us!...

The mystery has passed, I acknowledge it, and it happened only once, but the grace of it is not past for souls who prepare to have Jesus Christ born into their hearts. He was born once in Bethlehem, and He is born in our hearts every day through Communion, which is an extension of the Incarnation, as the Fathers say.

The reason the mysteries are re-presented to us by our Mother, the holy Church, is that we may be conformed to them by state, as much as we are able.[5] Meditate on and examine seriously the situations found in them in order to act in the same manner as Christians and members of Jesus Christ, our Head; for we will never be united to Him if we do not do the same things He did.

n. 2573, Chapter of December 17, 1671

Ask Our Lord today, when you will have received Holy Communion, that He Himself prepare your soul to be a pleasing dwelling for Him. You will ask me, since you receive Him today in all His majesty and grandeur just as on the day of Christmas, what difference is there from one Communion to another? I confess that it is always the same, but there is a particular grace attached to the mysteries at the times when they are presented to us by our Mother, the holy Church; and the more a soul is prepared, the more it participates in the grace of the mystery. Ask the Child Jesus for the portion He has reserved for you.

n. 316, Chapter in preparation for the coming of Jesus in us

---

[5] See 55, note 2.

We must never leave the Heart of Jesus in the Host: in it we receive the grace of all the mysteries, since they are all found in the Most Holy Eucharist. I find in it the mystery of the birth of Jesus; the mystery of the Circumcision; the mystery of the Epiphany, which is the manifestation of Jesus Christ. In short, we have His baptism, His hidden life, His public life—the Eucharist contains all the mysteries.

Of all that the holy Church possesses, this august Sacrament is the most divine.

n. 476, Conference for the vigil of Christmas

Adoration

I WOULD LIKE TO KNOW how you spend your hours of adoration before the Most Holy Sacrament, my Sisters. For you go before a God humbled and ennothinged for love of you, and who is not content to be adored in the Eucharist, but even more, who desires to be consumed. And as bread is the most nourishing food we have for the life of the body, and the one which we take most often, Jesus Christ my Savior gives Himself under the appearance of bread to be our food, and His desire is to be eaten by us, that we may live from His life as He lives from that of His Father.[1] You have the happiness to receive Communion so often; live from this divine life...

Jesus my Savior is in this adorable Sacrament not only to be adored there, but still more to be eaten. It is a dogma of faith that we eat the body of the God-Man, whom love holds captive under the species of bread and wine. And neither the malice of the wicked with all their rage, nor the insolence of libertines, has ever been able to make Him leave our tabernacles, so great is the love of Jesus Christ for us. Moreover, He says to us in the Gospel: "I will be with you till the end of the ages."[2] Here are, once more, the lengths to which my God's love for His creature goes.

n. 246, Conference to the novices, December 1687

Our Lord Jesus Christ gives His graces when one least expects it.

Regarding Communion, I have two thoughts. The first: since

---

[1] Cf. Jn 6:57.
[2] Mt 28:20.

Jesus Christ was continually offering reparation through Himself to the glory of His Father in the souls of the faithful, He alone was the true reparator, and what He was doing continually in the Most Holy Sacrament of the Altar is what He did once on the Cross during the three hours that He was on it. There He has perfectly and completely satisfied His Father's justice for the past, the present, and the future. I said to Him, "You yourself make reparation, since I am a sinner and therefore unable to do any good."

The second: we must forget ourselves entirely if we want to belong to Jesus Christ.

n. 2290, Essay

O adorable mystery—mystery of incomprehensible love! This is the feast of feasts, where God gives the whole of Himself, with all His infinite perfections, profusely and prodigally, more or less according as we will have taken care to prepare ourselves for it. And I dare to say that, all God and all powerful as He is, He cannot do anything more for His creature...

Our Lord has only two goals in all the divine and adorable mysteries which He effects: the first, to glorify His Father, and in second place, the salvation of men. But in the Eucharist, this divine lover of our hearts is hidden only for the love of His creature and will remain there even until the end of the ages... What more could He do, my Sisters? God Himself comes to the most intimate depths of our hearts. Why? In order to make us little gods and to make us by His grace what He is by nature. Do you want anything greater, holier, more divine?... Oh! My Sisters, what a blessing thus to possess this holy God, and how little known is the gift of God![3] Oh! If we had a little faith, where would we be?

A God gives Himself entirely to us through Holy Commun-

---

[3] Cf. Jn 4:10.

ion, all that He is and all that He has, as if He were not completely content and happy in Himself unless He possessed our hearts! Let us give them to Him, my Sisters, and through faithfully dying to ourselves, make Him our absolute Master...

My Sisters, let us go before this adorable Sacrament to learn our obligations. The Eucharist is the great book of life open to everyone, of which St. John speaks in the Apocalypse. It will instruct us and teach us all that we must do. How great are our blessings! Let us endeavor to profit from them. At all moments we can be offered with Jesus Christ; it is enough to be in a state of grace in order to be, in Him and through Him, continually immolated through the Holy Sacrifice of the Mass...

We have only to remain united in spirit and intention to Him, and we participate in the infinite merits of Jesus Christ; for though our sacrifice is a mere trifle, God's sacrifice attracts and merits for us an infinity of graces.

n. 188, Conference on Corpus Christi, 1683

Consider the relationship there is between us and Our Lord in the Most Holy Sacrament, together with all the virtues He exercises in it.

My Sisters, what kind of humility do we have? Where is the one among us who will be able to tell me that she sees the humility of Jesus Christ as the model of her own? It was said on the mountain, "Make it according to the model."[4] My Sisters, here is our divine model. Let us see if we are like Him. The eternal Father, in the Gospel, tells us, "Here is my beloved Son, hear Him."[5] Let us hear then, my Sisters, this divine Son and the lessons given to us by the divine preacher in this adorable Sacrament. There He gives us many lessons, first of humility, second of silence...

Let us go to the Most Holy Eucharist to learn to be quiet.

[4] Ex 25:40, Heb 8:5.
[5] Mk 9:7.

There, we see the Word of the Father, who says nothing, but we always want to talk...

It is not enough when you are in His divine presence to say with your lips, "My God, I adore you." That is something, but we must adore Him in spirit and in truth, namely, in our actions; this is what is called living by faith.[6] Do not say that it is too high for you; it is your obligation to live by faith and to be completely configured to Jesus Christ. We must not deceive ourselves; we promised to do this in baptism, and again in our religious profession. We must give an account of it one day, and we will be judged according to our good or bad execution of it. Say in all your actions, "I must do this as Jesus Christ did it when He was on earth. He is my example, I can have no other." Let us put ourselves once and for all into this spirit through serious reflection: my life must be conformed to that of Jesus Christ in the Most Holy Sacrament.

n. 1193, Chapter on the Presence of God

To adore a mystery so elevated above the lights of human reason draws upon us the divine good pleasure of God, who looks upon us with love. Therefore, go in a spirit of faith to the foot of the tabernacle, and let yourself burn in the divine presence of this God of love—there is nothing better you can do. But always present yourself with a deep humility because there is no disposition that honors God so much and glorifies Him more than our profound abasement. For, do not be mistaken about this, it is neither beautiful thoughts, nor lovely feelings, which make us pleasing to Him, but the true knowledge of ourselves...

Beware of letting the fire of His love go out in your hearts. I do not know how to repeat this enough to you, but, once more, let yourself burn in the presence of this God of love.

In order to be always in a state of adoration, it is not necessary

---

[6] Cf. Jn 4:23–24; Hab 2:4; Gal 2:20; Heb 10:38.

to say at every moment, "My God, I adore you." A single act suffices, and as long as you continue in the power of that act, you are in a state of adoration, provided you do nothing to the contrary. Accordingly, make only one act of adoration that continues always. Do the same with an act of humility, and strive to maintain it, for, if you want your adoration to be pleasing to God, it must always be accompanied by this holy virtue, which will draw down upon you His graces and make you worthy of divine union… Through Holy Communion, Jesus comes to communicate to you this divine life.

n. 1010, Chapter, April 29, 1695

We must be very surprised to see with what boldness people enter churches and we ourselves enter choir, which is a place sanctified by the Real Presence of God. Oh! If we could see the posture of the angels and the saints before the adorable Eucharist, we would not be so bold as to enter without fear, without respect, and without amazement. It is here that we lack faith.

n. 2176, Essay

Do not fail to adore the Most Holy Eucharist, which is the principal and the greatest devotion, and the one that all Catholics ought to have…. Perform your adoration, therefore, with more care and fidelity than ever, with a new fervor, ardor, and love for Jesus Christ in this precious mystery.

n. 138, Chapter, August 12, 1695

May Jesus in the Most Holy Sacrament of the Altar be our consummation!

Sir, the favor that was done for us of placing it [the Eucharist] in our chapel has taken away the leisure to reply sooner to your precious letter of the 23rd of last month. The consolation we have cannot be expressed, and I dare to assure you that He makes His Real Presence very much felt in this little house, for it seems to us that all the nooks and crannies are filled with Him, and we see His effects. However, we are not completely set up. Although we are housed, we do not have the cross, but we are in no hurry for the rest; it is enough that we have God in the Most Holy Sacrament.[7] We must carry our cross within as well as to the door of the monastery.

n. 1864, to M. Roquelay, April 10, 1653

My spirit sees you often before the august Sacrament, where I know you are as much as possible in order to pour out your heart in continual adoration of this God who is all love, ennothinged in the Host. Oh! What marvels are found in this ineffable Sacrament! There Love makes every effort and seems unable to find an invention with which to be manifested to mankind more mercifully. The Church presents us with this God of majesty in the precious womb of a virgin; let us adore Him there with amazement beyond words...

Strive, my dear daughter, to love this adorable Child who is nothing but love, and who loves you with an infinite love. Ask the most holy Mother of God to give you her love with which to love Him in the manger and in the Most Holy Sacrament of the Altar.

n. 2203, to Madam de Forax, December 1661

Jesus is that divine and royal eagle who rises to the throne of God through the hypostatic union; He contemplates, adores, and

---

[7] The cross in question is the cross erected on the outer wall or principal door of a monastery of nuns to indicate that the monastery has been canonically erected and that the enclosure has been established. The cross was at first refused by the Reverend Father Prior of the Abbey of Saint-Germain-des-Prés (who had authority over the territory in which the house was located) because in his estimation the nuns had insufficient income to ensure their living. It was only after the Countess of Châteauvieux obtained the required funds from her husband that the cross could be erected.

comprehends the divine perfections contained in the essence of God.[8] In the Most Holy Eucharist, He is doing His mysterious work, giving to the august Trinity an infinite homage and glory. We are little baby birds only fluttering on the ground without the power to take flight toward that infinite and supreme majesty to contemplate its grandeurs. We must slip under the wings of that Eucharistic eagle in order that, through His flight and the ardor of the beating of His wings, we may be elevated even to divine union, and admire and adore this sun—the essence of God—which cannot be understood or looked at fixedly, except by Himself. When we are before this sacramental majesty, we should remain, as I said, under the wings of Jesus Christ and do as He does with regard to His Father, by a union of intention or by a union of conformity and transformation or deification, according to the state and degree of love that each soul has. Spending entire hours this way in His holy presence, without other thoughts or interior acts, is in no way time wasted.

After receiving Communion, *He* should be our tongue for praising, blessing, exalting, adoring, and thanking His Father, and in the same way, our heart for loving Him. Jesus Christ does everything in a soul who allows Him to act—the secret is to remain in Him, striving not to leave Him. That is rare because of the mind's quickness and lightness. It runs after trifles and is filled sometimes without the soul noticing when something has entered the mind, and this obscures God's ray or disturbs the heart, drawing away the thoughts and attention.

n. 1535, *Conference*

---

[8] As the Son of God made flesh, Jesus is One of the Holy Trinity, sharing the divine essence with the Father and the Holy Spirit; there is no separate man to be taken up to God through the hypostatic union, as the language of the "divine and royal eagle" here suggests. We may say that Mother Mectilde is speaking freely, with poetic license, about the exaltation of human nature in the Incarnate Word.

United in Prayer

MADAM, THE DESIRE that I had to satisfy your devotion has delayed the present letter much longer than it should have. I assure you that your great devotion towards the Most Holy Sacrament of the Altar gives me a singular consolation. I have all the more joy from it because I think it makes up for the fidelity lacking in us to give the homage we owe to the divine Sacrament. I do not doubt, Madam, that you will receive very great graces from it and your holy daughters also. We have enrolled all the names of persons you have had the kindness to send us.

With all my heart I would like to be able to send you some nuns to contribute to your great fidelity to the Rule and to your piety, but I do not think it can be done this year, since we have been obliged to send some to Poland, where we have a monastery founded by the Queen of Poland. They left eight or ten days ago; I recommend them to your holy prayers. Their voyage is not on the sea at this time: there is too much danger because of the wars. They will suffer many hardships by land, having to cover close to 500 leagues of roads.[1] You would have been edified to see them depart with so much joy at being offered to Our Lord to go to increase His glory in the holy mystery of His love.

Madam, be so kind as to send word to me whether or not you can wait until next year. In the meanwhile, we can send you something about our customs, as much about perpetual adoration as about regular observance. I maintain a real desire to contribute as much as possible to your pious aspirations, and I assure

---

[1] One league = 4 km or 2½ miles; so, 2,000 km or 1,250 miles.

you that with all my heart I desire to be in Jesus and His holy Mother...

n. 1956, *to the abbess of the Benedictines of the Holy Trinity of Dorat, September 3, 1695*

Ladies, with an incredible consolation we have seen that it has pleased your goodness to do us the honor of writing to us about the impressions of love, homage, and reparation that the grace of Jesus caused in your hearts in regard to His divine and most adorable Sacrament.

It is impossible for us to express our joy to you, ladies, not doubting that the love of this sacred mystery makes you find most holy inventions to procure Him glory...

We have respectfully noted your names in the book of our association, at the same time beseeching Our Lord Jesus Christ to write you in His Heart and to make us worthy to be united to you for the glory of His divine Sacrament.

n. 2331, *Letter to a community*

May the Most Holy Sacrament of the Altar be praised forever!

We, Sister Mectilde of the Blessed Sacrament, humble prioress of the Benedictine nuns consecrated to the perpetual adoration of the Most Holy Sacrament of the Altar, of the Monastery of Paris, Superior of all the monasteries of the congregation of the same title of the Most Holy Sacrament: according to our power granted to us by the Holy See to associate all of the faithful, both men and women, in the perpetual adoration of this august mystery, entreat the Reverend Father Adrien Michel, most worthy religious of the strict observance of St. Francis of the city of Rouen, to assist us in this pious plan, which tends only to the glory of Our Lord Jesus Christ profaned by ungodly people in His Sacrament of love, and, on this account, to employ his zeal and piety in order to attract to it adorers, and giving to him all our powers to associate those (both men and women) that he will find able and disposed to this holy devotion and to take their names, the days and hours that they will choose in order to assist before the Most Holy Sacrament in a spirit of adoration and reparation, and to send these names to us, if he please, that they may be enrolled and entered from that time in association with our congregation and participate in all the good works, supplications, prayers, reparations and so on, which are practiced by the grace of God in all the monasteries of our Institute.

Given at our said monastery of Paris, August 7, 1661.

Sr. Mectilde of the Blessed Sacrament, Prioress,
(Autograph at Rouen)

May the Most Holy Sacrament of the Altar be praised and adored forever!

We, Sr. Marie Anne of St. Magdalene, humble prioress of the Monastery of Benedictines of Perpetual Adoration of the Most Holy Sacrament of the Altar, of the city of Toul, by request of the Reverend Mother Claude Apoline Richard, superior, and her community of nuns of the Visitation of St. Marie du Pont at Mousson, Madam the Marquise of Blainville, and Miss Claude la Pierre, her lady's maid, who desire to be associated in the perpetual adoration of the Most Holy Sacrament of the Altar and to be admitted to the participation in the spiritual goods that are practiced in our Institute: we, in consideration of their piety and singular devotion towards this adorable Mystery, according to the power granted to us by the Holy See to associate all the faithful, have associated and do associate by this [document] the said Madam de Blainville and her maid in order that they may have a share in the acts of amendment, reparations, adoration, prayers, supplications, penances, Communions, and generally in all the good works which are always practiced in our congregation, as if they were incorporated into it and made victims of the Son of God in His mystery of love, and asking humbly for reciprocal participation in all their prayers and good works, in testimony of which is the above, for which we have caused to be drawn up the present document for them, signed by our hand and countersigned by our secretary and affixing the seal of our monastery of the Holy Sacrament.

Sr. Marie Anne of St. Magdalene, Prioress,

by order of our reverend Mother Prioress,

Sr. Marie Anne of the Conception,

Secretary of the Chapter of our Monastery of the Holy Sacrament.

Monastery of Toul, this day August 14, 1684.

Worship and Devotion

Y ou know, my Sisters, that tomorrow is our greatest feast. I say that it is the greatest of all our feasts: it is a feast of the joy and triumph of Jesus in the Eucharist. Tomorrow the sacred Host is carried in ceremony and triumph—not only in Paris but throughout Christendom, where there are cities in which even more magnificence is displayed. The streets are adorned and there are richly decorated street altars; this little Host is carried under the canopy with respect and honor. Must this not truly give us joy, since we have a greater share in this holy mystery?

The Church, filled with the Holy Spirit, has chosen this day to honor the Most Holy Sacrament, and it can be said that she rejoices, seeing the faith of Catholics exercised. Yes, tomorrow faith shines forth, confessing that in this little Host God is present with all His majesty, and there is no day in the year when the faith of Catholics is more manifest...

Recently a letter was read to me that an Iroquois nun wrote to her director, who is here. To express the sentiments of respect she had for him, she says, "I put my face in the sand" (this is an expression of that country), out of the respect she has for his presence. I said to myself, "If one creature has so much respect for another, what should we have for God?" Let us do like this good nun, my Sisters. Let us put not only our head in the dust, but our entire body; let us prostrate ourselves before the majesty of God, who reduces Himself to a speck in order to come to us.

n. 3140, Conference for the feast of Corpus Christi

We should regard that glorious seraph, St. Michael,[1] as the guardian of the Most Holy Eucharist, since against Lucifer he supported the plan of the Incarnation of the Word. And if, in that moment, he gave Him homage and adoration, why should we not say that He is still the defender and guardian of the Most Holy Sacrament of the Altar, which is an extension of the Incarnation?

n. 136, Conference for the feast of St. Michael

All our troubles are from a lack of attention, and I exhort you— every time you feel stirred up and you want to express your feelings or speak some word of rebuke—that you say beforehand, "May the Most Holy Sacrament be praised forever." I assure you that you will not fall into so many faults, for the first impulse will have passed. One "Jesus, Mary" is enough to recollect your mind. I have said it to you before, and I repeat it often, but you make nothing of it; my words have more effect outside [the house] than within. I said the same thing some time ago to a person who was completely filled with and possessed by very violent passions. He complained of this to me, and I said to him, "Sir, try to make a good Confession and Communion, and when you feel this passion arise, say, 'May the Most Holy Sacrament be praised forever.'" He resolved to do this, and he put it into practice so well that he does not experience these passions anymore, not even knowing what has become of them, and he lives very happily at present. It is your prayers, my Sisters, which brought about this change, for I strongly recommended him to you, but we must attribute it all to the Mother of God, who is the Mother

---

[1] Although St. Thomas considered that St. Michael belonged to the second lowest order of angels, many theologians in Church history, including Aquinas's contemporary St. Bonaventure, maintained that Michael stood in the highest order, that of the seraphim (his identification as "archangel" being taken, then, in a more general sense: chief among angels).

of mercy. She shares this precious quality with her divine Son, interceding ceaselessly for sinners.

n. 2374, *Conference for the vigil of the birth of the Mother of God*

Countess: What is better when one has Masses said: to have particular intentions and tell them to the priest, or to have no others than those of the Church, and to join one's intention to that of the sacrifice?

M. Mectilde: The intention of the sacrifice and of the Church is very holy; you can honor and respect them, uniting yours to them. But you are permitted to have particular intentions sometimes and to tell them to the priest. You can also offer them yourself according to your secret and personal intentions, for the needs of your soul, or for the dead, or for the needs of some affair, or for your neighbor, and also for the pure interests of God, asking for the establishment of His reign in you, the grace to know Him, or to honor some saint to whom you have had recourse, or in thanksgiving for some mercy, etc. You can do the same with Holy Communion.

But always note that the Holy Sacrifice of the Mass sacrifices you with Jesus Christ; that you must be a victim and have a desire to surrender yourself to the designs of Jesus; that you enter into this spirit of victimhood, wholly immolated to the glory of the Father, the Son, and the Holy Spirit. At Communion, your sacrifice is still more complete, for you consent to it in fact, making room in yourself for the three divine Persons so that they may have power and authority in you, and you subject yourself to their divine sovereignty, surrendering yourself unreservedly to Jesus Christ.

n. 307, *Conversation with the Countess of Châteauvieux*

Let us go back to this poor soul, and tell me if she is elderly or not, and if it is a long time that she has been unyielding toward the things of her salvation, and how this miserable state came about. You must put her in the hands of the most holy Virgin at your next Communion.

n. 997, to Mother Gertrude of St. Opportune, April 17, 1690

I thank you for the Holy Communion that your charity, or rather, the charity of Jesus Christ, caused you to make for me. I beg you, continue to give me the part in your prayers which I hope for. My needs are extreme.

n. 311, to the Countess of Châteauvieux

I am going to have some prayers said for you, without your name being mentioned, and have some Masses said, in order to obtain the dispositions necessary for you to do this action with the perfection with which it should be done for your salvation. In the meanwhile, take heart, I expect that all will go well.

n. 31, to M. de Montigny

Let us allow God to act. All that I ask you, by means of the good priests who sometimes go on retreat in your holy hermitage, is that some Masses be offered which I am obliged to have said, according to particular intentions which have been given to us for that reason.

n. 383, to Jean de Bernières, 14 July 1651

I will use the gold Louis[2] that you sent me for some Masses for the repose of the soul of His Lordship the Marquis. He has need of aid, but he is very happy to have need of it. I deem it a great mercy that he is in purgatory, because his eternity is secure; you will relieve him by your prayers and your Holy Communions.

n. 490, to the Marquise of Raffetot

---

[2] Also called Louis d'or: gold coin circulated in France from 1640 until the Revolution.

I want to be God's more than ever, and I want to withdraw as much as possible from the bustle; that is why I need your help. Pray for me with all the fervor of your heart, and ask for my conversion. I entreat you: have some Masses said for this intention, for there is no longer a likelihood of my living without being God's entirely, without being engulfed in His Heart, drowned in His love, and completely ennothinged in the great All.

n. 1182, to M. Roquelay, January 9, 1643

Have some Masses said for your intention when you feel overwhelmed. It is a good thing to have recourse to the divine remedies and also to the holy angels. I hope that you will be delivered from this affliction. Have a little patience, courage, and trust.

n. 1217, to M. de Montigny

I was not able yesterday to have the consolation of writing to you to express my gratitude for the pains you have taken to obtain something substantial for me in support of the monastery of these good mothers of the Congregation of Our Lady, from Vezelize in Lorraine. It is a labor directly for the Most Holy Sacrament and sustains the honor given to Him in that house: the Holy Sacrifice and other pious works performed there. Do not doubt that Jesus in the Most Holy Eucharist is giving you rich rewards.

In this way you can obtain glory for Him, and on similar occasions you have glorified Him. You promised Our Lord to do Him honor in all the ways that will be shown to you, as much as you can, through yourself or through others. However, when you cannot do so by yourself, God desires that you prompt persons over whom you have some influence to do something for Him. Be unremitting in this. Never say: "That is enough," because it is for the God of infinite majesty, for the One to whom you owe everything and who deserves that we expend ourselves continually for His love and in His service. Therefore, when you cannot do anything for His glory, and when means are lacking to you by yourself, stir up others to do something in honor of this adorable Majesty hidden in the adorable Sacrament, this God who is all good, whom love keeps there for you, in order to give Himself to you and draw you to Himself. Oh! How happy you will be in heaven to have honored Him on earth! To whom do you give, and who causes you to give? It is Jesus Christ. He will be grateful to you and will repay a hundredfold. Oh! If I had the power, I would like to establish the praise, the adoration, and the glory of the Most Holy Sacrament of the Altar over the entire world. It is a great honor that He does to you, dearest lady—both to you and to me—to make use of us in such a noble cause. Therefore, on these occasions, work according to your ability.

n. 1144, *to Madam de Forax*

We received what it pleased you to honor us with, for which we have reason to bless Our Lord for the zeal for His glory in the august Mystery of our altars with which He has filled your heart. We cannot admire enough the graces with which He has animated you by His Spirit to find means to exalt Him in repairing the outrages that you know are done to Him every day. Alas! Sir, throughout the whole world there are godless people who endeavor to destroy Jesus Christ in the divine Eucharist...

May it please His goodness to animate many people with your zeal, who seek, like you, the means to have Him adored! I share the sentiments with which the Holy Spirit has inspired you . . . and if I could give my life to repair what is done by the enemies of that adorable Sacrament in your city, I would be at the height of supreme happiness. But I do not see any means of attaining this, if your goodness does not make use of its credit with God and men to succeed in this. I beseech you, with all possible ardor and respect, to work generously for a design which seems advantageous for the glory of our august Mystery.

Have the kindness to tell me how you think it will be in my

power to aid your holy intentions, and I will execute the orders that you give me, if it pleases Our Lord to favor me with His grace...

I close this letter, humbly asking for a share in your holy sacrifices.

n. 2319, to a priest

Jesus Christ, Our Lord, was supposed to make His entrance into His house. The next day, the feast of All Saints, she [Mother Mectilde] said, as if all in amazement: "What inconceivable goodness in Our Lord, to want to dwell with us! Oh! How great a day is tomorrow, a great feast for us! Let all that is most beautiful, most magnificent, be brought, so that I may adorn the altar with it. I am truly astonished that from every part of the world is not brought all that is most rich and rare to put upon the altar. What! When kings make their entry into their towns and kingdoms, every sort of pomp is prepared to receive them. And what! My God will come to dwell among some poor little wretches and paltry creatures, and no one thinks about this? It is amazing. I cannot bear it, and I do not know how to be astounded enough at these Jansenists who do not want to adorn their altars. We see that God Himself demonstrated a desire for it, since we observe, in the temple that God had built by Solomon, that the latter requested of Him to say all that He thought should be put there, even to an urn, that is, to the smallest thing."[3] She said these words in a manner so moving and loving that she truly expressed the feelings of her good heart.

Catherine de Bar, Fondation de Rouen,
Rouen 1977, p. 57

---

[3] According to 1 Chron 28:10–19, King David received from the Lord and then passed on to his son the plan of the Temple yet to be built, which calls to mind the exact instructions given by God to Moses for the building of the tabernacle (cf. Ex 25:9 et seq.).

The following text was written by Mother St. Joseph de Montigny-Laval to Mother Mectilde, on June 14, 1675, after the new chapel of the Benedictines of Perpetual Adoration in Nancy had been dedicated.

Finally, my reverend and dearest Mother, you have given to God a temple in which I think He will be truly honored. On Wednesday, the vigil of the feast of the Most Holy Sacrament, at nine o'clock in the morning, He was carried in procession with great solemnity by our Father Superior. The governors and stewards and all the principal officers attended, all the important men of the city in a body, and all the most important people in Nancy. There were more than twenty children dressed as angels with censers, a great number of ecclesiastics vested in copes and dalmatics. All the people from the neighborhood of our great church prepared the streets with carpets, paintings, and bonfires. At the sides of the streets, the pavement was strewn with flowers. All the workers who had labored on the church, being furnished with arms, were ranged in a row to allow the procession to pass, and at the moment when the Blessed Sacrament entered the church, they fired a great salute. Our organist played the music, which was as beautiful as one could have had in this place. Then the solemn Mass was chanted. The church and the surrounding eight side chapels were completely full, as well as the choir. It was the same at Vespers and Benediction.

On the day of Corpus Christi, the ministers of the bishop entered our church with the general procession, which has never been done before in the city of Nancy. The organ was played until the Blessed Sacrament was placed on the altar; then our most beautiful voices sang the *Ecce Panis*, which was deemed magnificent. Afterwards, Benediction was given. Our church, the entire day, was always full, from five in the morning up until seven o'clock in the evening. Everyone confessed that this place inspires devotion. One is so charmed with the beauty of this church that you are highly praised and blessed to have placed the final perfection on so beautiful a work. I know that you have only in view the glory of God in this enterprise, which costs you a great deal in many ways. You would have rejoiced to see your desires accomplished in this great solemnity. You were missing in our joy, which would have been perfect if we could have had you with us.

We are united to all your intentions, asking Our Lord for all that we have thought to be most for His glory in this adorable mystery, and for the perfection of our Institute. We will continue to ask Him with great earnestness for your health, which I hope He will grant us.

Prayers

Act of Oblation to Jesus in the Holy Eucharist

Divine and adorable Jesus,
I believe in You, and I adore You,
and I contemplate You in this mystery of love
as the holy and sacred Host
that bears and takes away the sins of the world,
and Who are here immolated by Yourself
for the glory of God Your Father
and for the salvation of men.

I learn from Your Apostle
that You desire that we all be living victims,[1]
holy and worthy of being sacrificed with You
for the glory of Your divine Father.

O my adorable Jesus!
In honor of and in union with the oblation and sacrifice
that You made of Yourself to Your Father,
I offer myself to You to be perpetually
a victim of Your most gracious will,
a victim immolated for Your pure glory.

Unite me to You.
Draw me into Your sacrifice
that I may be sacrificed with You and by You.

[1] Rm 12:1.

104

Cause me to die to myself and to all that displeases You.
Consume me entirely in the fire of Your divine love,
and make it so that henceforth my whole life
may be a continual sacrifice of praise, glory, and love
to Your divine Father and to You.
Amen.

n. 363

✝ ✝ ✝

For the Feast of the Presentation

Adorable Jesus, make me,
through Your Incarnation,
a pure victim with You,
through Your Presentation
a holy victim,
and through Your death on the Cross
a spotless victim;
that I may never be separated from You,
since, without You,
I cannot be pure, holy, or spotless.
Apart from You
there is only evil and corruption,
because the soul that is not united to You
is united and bound to itself,
to creatures, and to sin,
which can only cause evil in us.

Pray to the most holy Virgin to give you her divine Child, as she
did to the good Simeon; pray that she make us see, as he did, the
eternal Light. May He be today the sun of your soul forever, so
that you may walk in the truth: *Ego lux mundi*. He says: "I am the
light of the world. He who follows Me does not walk in dark-

ness."[2] Therefore, revere Jesus as the Light, so that, enlightening you with His sacred rays, you can follow Him at every moment of your life, and you may be pure victims through Jesus, holy victims through Jesus, and spotless victims through Jesus. Amen.

n. 459

Divine Jesus,
I unite myself to the grace
of Your divine sacrifice.
You are my victim, and I am Yours—
or better, I am one single victim with You.

I offer You to Your eternal Father for myself,
and I offer and consecrate myself to You
in order to render You endless thanksgiving
for all the mercies I receive
from Your adorable goodness
in this august mystery of the Holy Mass.

My God, I desire what You desire,
I desire to love You, to live only for You.
I renounce and abjure everything in me
that is opposed to You.

Live and reign, Jesus,
for You are my King,
and I desire with all my heart
to belong to You eternally.

My God, I intend and desire,
at each beat of my heart,

[2] Jn 8:12.

to adore, to love,
and to accomplish perfectly
Your most holy will.

n. 2196

✝ ✝ ✝

My divine Savior,
I know that ever since You have made
of Your precious flesh a Eucharistic bread,
You can no longer be without desires;
and consequently,
without making it seem that something is lacking
for the satisfaction of Your Heart.

This infinite ardor—
I can speak of it this way—
made You desire union with men
through this mystery,
which love has instituted
to draw them to participate
in all that You are in Yourself.

You were ennothinged
in the mystery of the Incarnation.
Was that not enough to satisfy You?
No, the love in You was not satisfied;
it wants to be ennothinged
in each soul in particular:
Desiderio desideravi.[3]

He desires to be consumed by us to establish His divine life in us,
so that, by this holy eating of His divine flesh, He may make us

---

[3] Lk 22:15. With desire have I desired (to eat this pasch with you).

entirely one with Himself; and by this means, He communicates to us all that He is as God, exalting us to share in the divine nature. Jesus Christ in the Most Holy Sacrament keeps this desire for us; He is still not satisfied. He will say unto the end of the ages: *Desiderio desideravi*. As long as there is a soul on earth capable of His grace, He will have an infinite desire to attract it to His love, that with it He might eat the Eucharistic Passover!

Oh! Whoever could hear or in the slightest way understand the ardor of Jesus would die from it out of amazement, seeing the excess of His divine charity. It is not that He has need of us for His Father's glory, but rather that He loves us in truth; He does not value His blessedness if we have no part in it. And since He looks upon us as members of His mystical Body, He cannot be satisfied if we are not united to Him and transformed into Him. Gazing at us from His Eucharistic throne, He cries out regarding us, *Desiderio desideravi*.

Let us hasten, then, let us hasten to the Most Blessed Sacrament! Let us go in order to satisfy the infinite desires of that adorable Heart. Let us receive Communion in order to please Him and satisfy those ineffable desires. Let us cast ourselves, unconditionally, at His sacred feet, saying to Him with a reciprocal love, the most ardent love possible for us:

O divine Heart!
O loveable Heart!
O Heart
whose excellence and goodness
are beyond words!
Satisfy Your desires in me;
draw me entirely to You
to fulfill Your desires.
Feed me in Your way
that I may be sustained with You,
and that Your desires

may find complete satisfaction.
Communicate to my soul
some small share
in Your ardent desires,
so that I may say,
every day in Communion,
with the same heart and the same love,
through the pouring out
of Your sacred desires in me:
Desiderio desideravi.

n. 594

+ + +

Act of Adoration of the Most Blessed Sacrament of the Altar

My God and my Savior, Jesus,
true God and true man,
worthy victim of the Most High,
living Bread, and wellspring of eternal life!

I adore You with all my heart
in Your divine Sacrament,
with the intention of making reparation
for all the irreverences, profanations, and sacrileges
commited against You in this aweful mystery.

I kneel before Your divine Majesty
to adore You now,
in the name of all those
who have never paid You any homage,
and who, perhaps, will be so unfortunate
as never to render it to You,
such as heretics, atheists,

blasphemers, sorcerers,
Jews, idolaters, and all infidels.

My God, I wish to be able to give you
as much glory as they all together would give you
if they faithfully gave You their reverence and gratitude.
And I wish to be able to gather into my faith,
my love, and the sacrifice of my heart,
all the honor, love, and glory
they would be capable of giving You
throughout all the centuries.

With all the fervor of my soul,
I desire to give You
as much benediction and praise
as the damned will spew of insults against You
throughout the duration of their punishment.

And in order to sanctify this adoration
and make it more pleasing to You,
O my Savior,
I unite it to all the adoration
of Your universal Church,
in heaven and on earth.

Look to the intentions of my heart
rather than to the words of my mouth.

To honor You, I would say to You
all that Your Spirit inspires
in your holy Mother and in Your saints,
and all that You Yourself say to God Your Father,
in this glorious and august Sacrament
where You are His perpetual holocaust,

and in the blessed Bosom
where He begets You for all eternity,
where You praise Him infinitely
through the Divine Essence.
Amen.

This prayer was published by the order of the Benedictines consecrated to the perpetual adoration of the Most Blessed Sacrament of the Altar and for the people associated with them, by the authority granted to them by the Holy See, in the adoration of that august mystery, and who became participants in the homage and other honors they offered day and night to that divine Sacrament in reparation for outrages received by the Son of God. To recompense this adoration, the Holy Father Pope Clement X (1670–1676) granted a plenary indulgence to the faithful who would [by praying it] unite themselves to the intentions of these Benedictines.

Mectilde of
the Blessed Sacrament
and Her Times†

Canon G. A. Simon
Priest Oblate of St. Wandrille Abbey

O NE DAY in the spring of 1639, a young nun presented herself at the Monastery of the Benedictine Nuns of Rambervillers, where she was expected. She wore the habit of the Order of the Annunciation. The young woman appeared to be of remarkable distinction, her face was both noble and gracious, her manner easy. The nun who received her in the parlor was struck by this grace and nobility, and when the visitor began to speak to her with an amazingly harmonious voice, she rose suddenly and, hurrying to find the Mother Prioress, declared to the sisters whom she found on the way, "Oh! It is the nun I saw, my Sisters! Oh! The beautiful nun! We are only beguines in comparison." The Prioress, Mother Bernardine of

---

† In preparing this portrait, the author consulted the following sources: Arnaud-Bernard d'Icard Duquesne,*Vie de la Vénérable Mère Catherine de Bar dite en religion, Sœur Mechtilde du Saint-Sacrement, institutrice des religieuses de l'Adoration perpétuelle* (Nancy: Lamort, 1775); Canon Hervin and Marie Dourlens, *Vie de la Très Révérende Mère Mechtilde du Saint-Sacrement* (Paris: de Bray et Retaux, 1883); idem, *Vie abrégée de la Trés Révérende Mère Mechtilde du Saint-Sacrement* (Paris: de Bray et Retaux, 1883); *Catherine de Bar, Mère Mechtilde du Saint-Sacrement*, Publication bénédictine "Pax" (Montauban: Prunet, 1922); two manuscript biographies kept in the monastery of the Benedictines of Bayeux.

the Conception, came almost immediately. She had a short conversation with the visitor. The door of the cloister was opened, and the visitor disappeared into it.

This nun, who in this way came to have a first contact with the monastery of Rambervillers, was called in religious life Mother St. John the Evangelist. Although she was only twenty-five years old, she had filled, for more than three years, the office of deputy manager of the monastery of the Annunciades of Bruyères, about six leagues from St. Dié.[1]

In the world, her name was Catherine de Bar. She was born in St. Dié, in a house which today is 27 Thiers Street, on December 31, 1614. Her father, Jean de Bar, belonged to an ancient family of magistrates, famous in Lorraine for their ancient honor and solid piety.[2] Catherine was the third child of the marriage, which was to count six. Like her brother, Jean-François, who was destined to be a soldier, and her sisters—one married to Mr. de Champagne, Colonel of Infantry; another to Mr. L'Huilier, also Colonel and later governor of the Château de Bar; a third to Mr. Alix, civil Lieutenant to the Bailiff of St. Dié; and a fourth to Mr. de Vienville—she had received a very careful education, comprising Latin, painting, music, and so on, as was fitting for a young lady destined to live in the most distinguished society. She had also received, from parents animated with a fervent and intelligent piety, a solid religious formation.

When very young she felt the divine call and answered it as best she could. Having left to her father the choice of monastery in which she would give herself to God, after long months of refusal, he presented her in November 1631 to the Annunciades of Bruyères. Her postulancy completed, she received the novice's

---

[1] One league = 4 km or 2½ miles. Total distance: 15 miles.

[2] The de Bar family appears in the ancient armorial of Lorraine as having: on azure, in a band of silver with 3 crosses, recrossed and pointed with sable, accompanied by 2 gold *besans*, 1 heads and 1 tails (*Nobiliaire du duché de Lorraine et de Bar par le duc René* [Gand: Duquesne, 1862], 68).

habit there, with the name of Sr. St. John the Evangelist. After the year of novitiate was done, she pronounced her vows. Shortly after this profession, the Superior, Mother Angélique, having had to leave the monastery, asked Sr. St. John the Evangelist, barely twenty years old, to replace her, with the title of deputy manager, so evident was her maturity of judgment. The young professed tried everything to avoid this burden, imposed on her in the name of obedience. When, in 1635, the Thirty Years' War broke out, which was to put Lorraine to fire and sword, she had been governing her little flock in peace for almost two years.

In the first days of May 1635, the sisters had to evacuate their monastery quickly at the approach of the Swedish, who were feared for their ferocity. The monastery was destroyed by fire a few hours after their departure. There were given refuge at first at Badonvillers. When the community had to split up, Mother St. John and one of her companions, at the beginning of 1636, were welcomed at Commercy, by the Marquis of Armoises, who handed over to them one wing of his chateau, called the Château-Bas. She called her daughters there. After this, the plague broke out and, among twenty nuns, she was able to save only five. During these terrible days, Mother St. John was tried with terrible anxieties about her father, who had been arrested, taken to Obernai, and thrown into a dreadful prison. At the end of 1637, he was able to return to St. Dié, and proposed to his daughter that he settle her and the remainder of her community in a wing of the family mansion.

While all this was happening, a friend recommended the young Superior of the Annunciades to the Benedictines of Rambervillers, who knew through other connections Colonel L'Huilier (her brother-in-law), who had done them great services. The Prioress, Mother Bernardine of the Conception, with an entirely Benedictine generosity, responded, "Let her come." And it is thus that, accompanied by one of her daughters and some secular women, Mother St. John came to Rambervillers.

✝ ✝ ✝

The monastery of Rambervillers followed the Rule of St. Benedict, drawing its inspiration from the Constitutions which came
from Dom Didier de la Cour de la Vallée to the Congregation of
St. Vanne and St. Hidulphe, from which was to come the well-
known Congregation of St. Maur.[3] From the first moment, a
totally spontaneous sympathy united Mother Bernadine to her
young guest. She proposed that she stay for three weeks at the
monastery, then finally to stay there as long as she liked in a separate part, where, with some of her companions, she could follow her Rule. This was the first contact Catherine de Bar had
with the Benedictine order; it was to be decisive. In fact, she felt
little by little attracted by this Rule, older and more austere than
that of the Annunciades. She reflected at length, deliberated a
great deal, drew up a report that she addressed to Rome (the
bishopric of Toul being vacant at that time), and on July 2, 1639,
entered the novitiate of Rambervillers, where she was given the
name of Sr. Catherine of St. Mechtilde.

The novice mistress to whom she was entrusted, Mother
Benedicta of the Passion, was a nun about the age of thirty. In the
world, she was called Elizabeth Brem.[4] The Brems were known
for their traditional piety. Born in Saarbourg in 1609, Elizabeth
had been married at the age of seventeen to a fervent Christian,
Mr. Chopinel, who was an officer of the Primate of Lorraine.
Having become a widow at the age of twenty-three, she had
entered the Benedictines of Rambervillers.

Mother Benedicta of the Passion truly belonged to her age, in
which everything tended to be grand and things were not done

[3] Cf. Dom E. Didier Laurent, *Dom Didier de la Cour et la réforme des monas-
tères bénédictins lorrains 1550–1623* (Ligugé, 1900).

[4] We find a long *Eloge de la Vénérable Mère Elisabeth de Brême,* in J. de Blémur, *Eloges de plusieurs personnes illustres en piété de l'Ordre de Saint Benoît* (Paris,
1868), 2:1–112.

by halves. It was an epoch of great strokes of grace, of staggering conversions, of prodigies of mortification. Not only at La Trappe, which was to be the peak, but in the smallest reformed monasteries, severe austerities, hair shirts, and disciplines were appreciated and continued to be endorsed for a long time, for love of the Cross of Jesus and also in opposition to the excesses of the age. The monks of St. Vanne, just as the Maurists would do later, threw themselves avidly into everything that crucified body and soul. Mother Benedicta saw that her novice was a character of this mettle. She drew her to follow her in these austerities, which were certainly not in the Benedictine tradition, which is all discretion. In contrast, she discovered this discretion in the way in which her novice mistress initiated her into prayer. After having made Sr. St. John practice the current methods, Mother Benedicta, feeling she was called to contemplation, left her to follow the attractions of the Holy Spirit. She helped her though in her own way, which was a severe way: "She took away from her all of her books of piety, apart from her Breviary, her Rule, and some prayers: the method was successful for her. A single word from Scripture or from the Liturgy was enough for the novice to feed her soul and to be lost in God."

On July 11, 1640, on the feast of the Translation of St. Benedict, Catherine of St. Mechtilde, twenty-five years old, pronounced her vows. According to the notes that she drew up later, she asked on that occasion to be "so much dead and crucified to the world" that the world and all earthly things would be to her a "true cross." She made the resolution to be "deeply plunged in the consciousness of her nothingness, of her abjection and misery, that she might feel herself for her whole life as if under the feet of all creatures." That this was the core of her thought at that time cannot be doubted. With regard to the terms "nothingness" and "abjection," we believe that they entered into her vocabulary later, after she had been in contact with the mystics of Normandy.

✝ ✝ ✝

In that tumultuous epoch, Rambervillers was a very poor community indeed. The continual wars had reduced it to such an extreme of misery that, scarcely three months after the profession of Catherine de Bar, the sisters found themselves faced with the necessity of splitting up the community.

In the course of September 1640, accompanied by her dear Novice Mistress and one other nun, Mother Anne-Bernardine of the Presentation, Catherine of St. Mechtilde left for St. Mihiel, where a lady friend had offered to give them refuge. The town, which had been claimed by both the Austrians and the French, was completely ruined. The townspeople, who had turned the cannon on the carriage of Louis XIII and had killed many of his officers, had been ransomed at great expense, and at the same time they had seen their chateau and ramparts razed. Nevertheless, the three nuns were able to establish themselves in one of the little "cells" or temporary houses which were used in the town as refuges for monks and nuns who had been driven from their monasteries. There, they labored to keep their observances, and in order to be useful to the town and obtain some funds, they opened a little school.

Only with difficulty can we imagine the misery suffered then by the people in that region. Because of the war, the fields were empty and the soldiers had pillaged the last reserves. Those who did not die of hunger died of disease. In the midst of this complete destitution, the three Sisters heroically shared in the common trial: "We suffered a great poverty," Mother Mectilde would write later,

> but in the deprivation of everything necessary for life, Our Lord compensated us with such goodness that it seemed to us that we had nothing to suffer. For me, in particular, I was so flooded with consolations that I sometimes found myself obliged to entreat Our Good Master to moderate

them. We lived in great peace and perfect union, following our observances as if we had been in our monastery.

In Paris, the charitable Vincent de Paul, unceasingly on the watch to help those in distress, multiplied collections and sent provisions and clothing to the suffering areas. One day, one of his followers, Mr. Guérin, came knocking at the door of the nuns' poor little temporary house. The small community who welcomed him was in a condition of shocking raggedness, the clothing in tatters, the faces bearing the traces of long privation. He judged that the situation could not continue. In agreement with the grand vicar of Toul, he caused the nine sisters remaining at Rambervillers to come to St. Mihiel, with the intention of dispersing the twelve nuns into various Benedictine abbeys. The sisters from Rambervillers arrived around Easter 1641, led by Mother Bernardine of the Conception.

Mr. Guérin, who was returning to Paris, had intended to entrust some of the Sisters, including Mother Mectilde, to the abbess of Montmartre. At first he had received a refusal, then after a mysterious dream, the abbess changed her mind, and in the course of August 1641, the Sisters saw Mr. Matthew Renard arrive in St. Mihiel, sent by Vincent de Paul. "My Mother," he said to the Prioress [Mother Bernardine], "I have come to take two of your nuns, to escort them to Montmartre. I have the funding for the journey; the Duchess of Aiguillon has given it to me." The abbess asked expressly for Mother Mectilde. Mother Louise of the Ascension was sent as her companion. They left on the 21st of August.

✝ ✝ ✝

Marie de Beauvilliers, abbess of Montmartre, would have been a very great lady if she had stayed in the world. A fervent nun, she had remained a great lady, with all that this word implies of true grandeur of character and simple dignity in her interactions—a dignity and nobility that were reflected even in the features of her face, which were of great beauty, and in her extremely courteous manners.[5] She had entered religion very young, at the Abbey of Beaumont les Tours, and in 1598, at the age of twenty-four, had been called to the Abbey of Montmartre, which was truly the most wretched, the most lax, and the most disreputable in the kingdom. With a mixture of energy, tenacity, and sweetness, she had gradually led the nuns back to regular observance—they, who had begun by attempting to poison her and even once tried to have her assassinated. Thanks to the help of her family and especially her brother-in-law, Pierre Forget, Lord of Fresne, she had put order back into the temporal affairs. With regard to the spiritual, she had been greatly helped by the famous Capuchin and future martyr, Benedict of Canfield, and by Dom Didier de la Cour. She herself had given the example of poverty, humility, charity, and zeal for regular observance and the Divine Office. When Mother Mectilde was presented to the abbess, Montmartre, whose ancient ruined buildings still rose up in the midst of the woods and orchards,[6] was then justly known as one of the most fervent monasteries in France. "We enjoyed a profound peace there, and the hand of God was visibly on that holy mountain," wrote Madam de Blémur.[7]

---

[5] On Madam de Beauvilliers, see Mme de Blémur, *Eloges*, 2:143–84, and H. Bremond, *Histoire Littéraire du sentiment religieux*, 2:442–84.

[6] The basilica of the Sacred Heart occupies the site of one of these orchards. In her notice on *La dernière Abbesse de Montmartre* (Coll. Pax, 1921), Madam Delsart has well summarized the monumental history of the Abbey.

[7] de Blémur, *Eloges*, 2:170. Madam de Beauvilliers, said Mother de Blémur, had printed, "an excellent volume of *The Explication of the Rule in the Form of a Dialogue between Master and Disciple*" (ibid., 2:174). We have perused in the past a simple *Explication* on the Rule of St. Benedict written in the form of a dialogue by R. P. M. D. B. R. B. (Paris: Brillaine, 1637). What do these letters signify? Under the initials M. D. B. R. B., should we not see Marie de Beauvilliers, Benedictine Religious?

Madam de Beauvilliers received the two travelers with the warmest cordiality; it was the same with the community. A few weeks later, Mother Mectilde could write to Mother Benedicta of the Passion:

> I have already wished more than a thousand times for you to be in this holy place where I am. . . . If there is a paradise on earth, I can say that it is Montmartre, where the virtues are practiced perfectly and our holy Rule is kept with a most exact observance. I know that in the past you thought it had not been reformed, but I can assure you and swear that it is applied perfectly here . . . so that it wins admiration, and I entreat you to praise and give thanks to our good God.

It was with an unspeakable emotion that Mother Mectilde prayed in the old crypt that had been discovered in 1611, and which was full of relics. But what moved her especially was the devotion of the abbess and the community to the holy Virgin. The abbess, Madam de Beauvilliers, had chosen Mary "as protectress of the house"; Madam de Blémur tells us that this choice "obligated her to place her statue in the middle of the choir, on the abbess's seat, holding a crosier in her hand, so that she received the honor given to the Superior and was viewed as the sovereign of all the nuns."[8] Was this in place when Mother Mectilde came to the Abbey? We know only that it was done before the *Fronde*, which began in 1648. However that may be, it testifies to a current of Marian piety in which the abbess and Mother Mectilde were to find a deep satisfaction.

Mother Mectilde would keep her time at Montmartre in unforgettable remembrance. She made holy friendships there with several exceptional nuns, especially with Charlotte Le Sergent, whose advice was to become for her a support in what fol-

---

[8] de Blémur, *Eloges*, 2:176.

lowed, especially at the foundation of the nuns of Perpetual Adoration.[9]

However, Madam de Beauvilliers was disturbed to see traces
of tears on the face of Sr. Mectilde. "Alas!" she told her one day,
"how can I rejoice to find myself so comfortable? Right now my
sisters may have nothing to eat!" Deeply moved, the abbess sent
word to Matthew Renard, who, a few days later, took the road
to St. Mihiel again, in order to bring back the seven nuns who
were still there. After a short stay at the Abbey, two of the Sisters, Mothers Madeleine of the Resurrection and Angélique of
the Nativity, left for Caen, where Madam Laurence de Budos,
another great reforming abbess, had offered to receive them at
her abbey of Holy Trinity. Scarcely installed at Holy Trinity,
Mother Angélique fell gravely ill. She did not want to die without seeing her dear Mother Mectilde again. At the same time,
through other channels, a little "hospice" was offered to the Sisters, situated about 20 km from Caen, near the Cistercian abbey
of Barbery. To the great regret of the abbess of Montmartre,
Mother Mectilde, accompanied by Mother Bernardine of the
Presentation and Mother Dorothy of St. Gertrude, left the
Abbey on August 7, 1642, feast of St. Lawrence, and on August
10, took the coach for Caen. On the 14th, the vigil of the
Assumption, the abbess of Holy Trinity, Madam de Budos,
received them with a familial cordiality.

The abbess was 65 years old; she was very petite, charming,
gracious, and spiritual. She had become abbess at thirteen, after
the death of the old abbess, who was her cousin, a Montmorency.
At twenty, she had undertaken the reform of her abbey, of which
both the temporal and the spiritual affairs left a great deal to be
desired. She had brought to this a tenacious will, a great deal of

---

[9] One account of Mother de Blémur, but without any author listed, is
Abrégé de la Vie de la V.M. Charlotte Le Sergent (Paris, 1685); cf. H. Bremond,
Histoire Littéraire, 2:467 ff.

patience and sweetness, and a profound supernatural under-standing. The result of her reform she recorded in a small book which has become extremely rare. It is *The Rule of the Religious Daughters of the Order of St. Benedict, Reformed in the Royal Monastery of the Holy Trinity at Caen*. It was printed in Caen in 1623 by Michael Yvon. The observance of the Rule was mitigated, but practiced with fervor. Mother Mectilde was able to see, on those feast days of the Assumption, what veneration Caen had for Our Lady. She also saw with what love the Holy Eucharist was sur-rounded, for which, as Madam de Blémur says, the abbess was "so hungry" that her confessor had to allow her to receive Com-munion almost every day.[10] For ten days, there were long exchanges of views between these two fervent nuns, and Madam de Budos conceived such a high regard for her visitor that she proposed to her—though in vain—to keep her as coadjutrix.

The temporary housing that had been offered to Mother Mec-tilde was found in the parish of Bretteville, in the valley of the Laize, on the edge of the forest of Cinglais. Upon arrival, it turned out to be a disappointment. There was only a thatched ramshackle cottage, without furniture, and in danger of flooding from the stream with every rainfall. Used to misery, Mother Mectilde moved in—for better or for worse—with Mother Angélique, who had become so feeble that she could not stand up anymore, and a secular girl who had accompanied them from Paris. While this was going on, a pious gentleman from the area passed along this road, Sir Jean de Morel, Lord of Torp, who was commonly called Mr. de Torp. He was brokenhearted at what he discovered and immediately offered the two nuns and their com-pany a little house which he owned near the abbey of Barbery. From that moment, together with his only daughter, Charlotte, wife of the Count François de Montgomery, he provided for all their needs.

---

[10] *Eloge de Madame de Budos*, in de Blémur, *Eloges*, 2:113 ff.

✝ ✝ ✝

The visit of Mr. de Torp was to have important consequences for Mother Mectilde. This gentleman was intimately connected with the Abbot of Barbery, Dom Louis Quinet, and both the one and the other were followers of and close friends with the great mystic of Caen, Jean de Bernières-Louvigny. Very close connections were to be created between Mother Mectilde and this fervent group.

The Cistercian Abbey of Barbery was, beginning in 1639, governed by Dom Louis Quinet,[11] who had reformed it with a patience and tact which recalled that of Madam de Budos.[12]

At the same period, Mother Mectilde had the occasion to visit the Benedictine Abbey of Vignats, which had just been reformed by Madam Anne de Médavy. The cloister buildings had recently been rebuilt around a great and beautiful church, of which today there is not a single stone left. The abbess, said a contemporary author, was a "lady of distinguished virtues . . . completely frank and cordial," and her community was a "true school of Jesus Christ Crucified."[13]

It is not immaterial to observe that all these connections were truly providential for Mother Mectilde, with these persons rep-

---

[11] He will publish in 1651 *Eclairissements ou Conférences sur la Règle de Saint Benoist* (Caen: Poisson).

[12] Cf. G. A. Simon, *Un mystique bénédictin normand: Dom Louis Quinet, Abbé de Barbery* (Caen: Jouan, 1927). On his rather strained relations with the Jansenists, consult Mother de Brégny, *Vie de la Mère Marie des Anges*, 195–219, for which we are indebted to Rev. Fr. du Chesnay, CJM (Eudist Father) and H. Bremond, *Les Illuminés de Picardie*, in *Vie Intellectuelle* (1931): 304–26. See also D. Quinet, *Les noviciat des Bénédictins* (Paris: Jean Pocquet, 1653). I was not able to find this work when I wrote my study about Dom Quinet. I became aware of it subsequently through the late D. Aubert de Boury, of the Abbey of Hautecombe.

[13] Cited by the Baron Angot des Rotours, *Françoise de Faudoas d'Averton*, 81–82.

resentative of the Benedictine reform, each animated with different nuances, but having the same zeal for the Rule and its exact observance.

In the meantime, Mr. de Torp and Dom Quinet did not cease to recommend to Mother Mectilde that she become acquainted with their common friend, Mr. de Bernières, whose authority in the religious world was great at that time, although he did not at all pose as a teacher.

Jean de Bernières-Louvigny, general treasurer of France in Caen, born there in 1602, was in fact one of the most notable people of the Catholic renewal. His name is connected with all the pious and charitable foundations of Normandy and elsewhere: the Oratory of Caen, the Ursulines, the Little Hermits, Our Lady of Charity in the same city, the Propagation of the Faith, the evangelization of Canada, and so on. The extension of the kingdom of God was the only passion of his life. There was not a soul more detached from the world, more interior, more lost in God than this man of action, involved in so many apostolic works.

In 1646–49, he built an enclosed retreat house, close to the convent of the Ursulines (which he had founded and his sister Jourdaine directed), where one could find bishops, monks, secular priests, and devout lay persons. A significant portion of 17th-century mysticism passed through those doors. Recourse was willingly had to the advice and direction of this founder, who counted among his directees even some nuns, though he accepted these only reluctantly. This retreat house was called the Hermitage. The bombings of 1944 completely destroyed what remained of the convent and the Hermitage at the end of Rue Singer.

The meeting of Mother Mectilde and Jean de Bernières was a very important date in her life. The solitary of Caen, whom she called her "very dear brother," would be a constant advisor and support for her in the important work which remained for her to bring to realization. Above all, she would enter fully into the current of spirituality that characterized the mystics of the Hermitage.

+ + +

Mother Mectilde stayed at Barbery only until 1643. She received at that time a letter from Fr. du Bonnefonds, a Jesuit, who, on behalf of Madam de Vallière, mother of one of the nuns of Montmartre, offered her a spacious and furnished house, situated at St. Maur les Fosses, in which she would be able to regroup part of her community. Mr. de Torp and Dom Quinet, despite their regret at seeing her go, advised her to accept, and the excellent gentleman [Mr. de Torp] paid for the expenses of the trip to Paris.

Mother Mectilde, who had taken as a companion Mother Bernardine of the Conception, was in Paris at the beginning of June 1643. While waiting till it was possible to move into the house in St. Maur, she lodged with some friends of Fr. du Bonnefonds. A continual exchange of letters kept her in contact with her friends in Normandy. These were very intimate, but were very quickly clouded by the death of dear Mr. de Torp, who had called Mectilde his "spiritual daughter."[14] It was during August 1643 that the two nuns moved into St. Maur. They called there the nuns of Rambervillers, who were to be found at Barbery, Jourarre, and St. Mihiel. From that time on, they felt themselves gradually surrounded by a network of warm affections. There were the nuns, such as Madam de Montmartre and the abbess of Chelles, Madam de Mailleraye, great ladies, and at their head, the greatest lady of the kingdom, Queen Anne of Austria, and many more, humbler and less known. The great Condé himself, who

---

[14] Seventy-three of these letters are known to us through an ancient copy (end of the 17th century) kept in the precious archives of the Benedictines of Bayeux.

was the lord of St. Maur des Fossés, took an entirely paternal care of the community. He visited them and even went into the kitchen to assure himself that they lacked nothing. The Sisters operated a boarding house for ladies of noble families. The little community very quickly took up again its regular observance, cloister, fasting, and so on. In the modest chapel where they were able to have Mass, the nuns chanted the choral office.

Toward the middle of 1645, an emaciated person of austere demeanor was presented in the parlor. This was again someone sent by Jean de Bernières, the singular Fr. Jean Chrysostom of St. Lô, penitent brother of the Third Order of St. Francis. For some years he was to direct Mother Mectilde—and through some rather severe paths. [15] It is difficult to imagine mortification more complete, without caution, almost without pity. "You are a father made of iron," one of his penitents told him. "The man is pitiless, nature no longer exists for him." But he set the example himself. [16] We must do him this justice: despite all his rigorism, Fr. Chrysostom taught that "it is necessary to allow souls a great liberty to follow the attractions of the spirit of God," especially in prayer. [17]

The first interview in the parlor was an illumination for Mother Mectilde. She wrote to Jean de Bernières in June 1645:

> My very dear brother, I have had the good fortune to see and to speak with him for about an hour. In this little time I made him acquainted with my past. . . . He gave me as

---

[15] On Fr. Chrysostom, one may consult the work of Henri Boudon, *L'Homme intérieur ou la vie de la Vénérable Père Jean-Chrysostôme, religieux pénitent du troisième ordre de Saint-François* (Paris: Michallat, 1684).

[16] Boudon, *L'Homme intérieur*, 204.

[17] Ibid., 283. [We must also add that a more recent biographer, Sr. Véronique Andral in *Itinéraire spirituel de Mère Mectilde*, argues that this picture of Fr. Chrysostom is distorted. In the documents we have of his direction of Mother Mectilde, he continually counsels her to prudence and discretion.—*Trans.*]

much consolation, as much courage about my life, and as much satisfaction about the state in which God keeps me as I could desire on earth. He is an angelic and heavenly man, through the singular effects of a very intimate grace that God pours into him.

Fr. Chrysostom, who lived in Paris, came often to St. Maur. Every six weeks, he gave conferences on his favorite subjects: prayer and mortification, and in particular bodily mortification. Mectilde, who had been gravely ill at Barbery, was far from having recovered. Did it matter? Mortifications rained down: sleeping on the bare floor, three hours of sleep, a belt studded with points, frequent use of the discipline, prolonged fasts, and so on. One could not resist this fearful man who spoke in the name of God. The penitent did not die from it. She even recovered completely, which allowed her biographers to say that Fr. Chrysostom acted through divine inspiration. We, however, must acknowledge that his direction was of a nature to warp the Benedictine perspective in Mother Mectilde, had she not, as if by instinct, in her growing attachment to the monastic Rule, returned of herself to moderation, so dear to St. Benedict.

In his own person, as we said, Fr. Chrysostom set the example, and it was he who ended by succumbing to it. Fr. Chrysostom died a most edifying death on March 26, 1646, after a moving visit of ten days at St. Maur, a stay that he had foreseen would be the last. Despite her deep faith, Mother Mectilde was for a short time distraught. She wrote to Jean de Bernières: "It's over. The sacrifice of our saintly Father is consummated. Despite all my satisfaction being in the accomplishment of the will of God, He nevertheless allows me to feel this loss keenly. Oh! It is a great sacrifice for you and me!" With Fr. Chrysostom gone, she wanted Bernières to take over in future the direction of her soul. "I can find no words to describe to you my sorrow, dearest Brother: have pity on me, for the love that the saintly Father bore you; be for me in this world what he was for me."

When the days of mourning were over, she experienced an impression of peace. "I feel," she wrote to Bernières,

> strengthened to go to God in the purity of His ways and through His own spirit. Jesus poor, suffering, and abject is the love of my heart at present. Supreme independence from creatures, sufferings without consolation from any creature; I must strive to practice this according to the degree of the grace given to me, as I can from this divine lesson.

+ + +

The year 1647 brought other trials to Mother Mectilde, with, it is true, the abundant consolation of regaining for a time her friends in Caen.

In that period, there was in Geôle Street—a street now crooked and decayed, which was then one of the most beautiful in the city—a little priory of Benedictine nuns, *Bon Secours*, recently founded by a noble woman of high piety, Madeleine de Moges, Marchioness of Mouy. Governed by a prioress of narrow piety, Mother Felicity Vion, the community was not flourishing. Consulted, Bernières and Dom Quinet found a solution right away: Mother Mectilde must go to the nuns!

The latter did not make an objection, but she submitted the decision to her superiors. "I would prefer, a thousand times over," she wrote to Bernières, "a little corner in my state of abjection than all the abbeys in France." It was proposed that she receive an abbess's crosier. Dom Quinet wrote to Rambervillers, where the community was partially regrouped, but stagnating in its wretchedness. This initiative was at first rejected, but when Madam de Mouy undertook to provide for the needs of the Sisters, the Prioress, Mother Bernardine, allowed herself to be swayed. The resignation of Mother Felicity was obtained and Mother Mectilde was elected by the community. During the discussions, she had had the occasion to demonstrate her attachment to obedience. Had not Dom Quinet, who was considered an oracle on the interpretation of the Rule, advised counseling her (it is not clear on the basis of what considerations) to come to Caen, even against the wishes of her Prioress? "If I were to do that," she wrote to Bernières,

> Madam de Mouy would have me driven out like a villain and an infidel, all the more since, through such a fault, I would draw on her house an infinity of curses. . . . The Abbot of Barbery may say what he likes, but as long as Our Lord keeps me through His grace, I would not yield to such advice.

The evening of June 28, 1647, Mother Mectilde arrived in Caen by coach. She was dressed in a worn tunic, for she wanted to enter the town "like a poor person, without being seen or recognized by anyone."

The new prioress made quick work of winning the hearts of her little flock. She did this by a mixture of sweetness and energy and by the impression she gave of an ardent love, delicate and attentive, and always supernatural, for each one of her daughters, who found in her a mother and a model. Moreover, she had the ability to discern spirits to a great degree. In a few months, the community was transformed.

During these three years, the communication with the Hermitage, it is understood, was constant. As we said, it is beyond question that Jean de Bernières' influence was considerable. But it is doubtless providential that Mother Mectilde found near to him Dom Quinet, whose monastic spirit would temper, in the Benedictine sense, anything found to be a little exclusive in the teachings current at the Hermitage. Certainly, the provisional Prioress of Caen could find in the Rule an invitation to the life of prayer and the chapter on humility could teach her holy abjection. However, at the Hermitage, abjection seemed to be sought for its own sake, whereas in St. Benedict it is welcomed only as it presents itself, as one of the means to arrive, by way of the twelve degrees of humility, at perfect love. Dom Quinet also certainly preached the ways of prayer, to which he devoted his *Treasure of Piety*, which came out precisely in 1648. Thus it was extremely helpful to Mother Mectilde to find on her path the Abbot of Barbery, to keep her in the way of monastic spirituality.

The year of respite once past, the Prioress had to leave the monastery of *Bon Secours*, despite the sadness of her daughters, to go to Rambervillers, where the community had elected her Prioress. Before leaving Normandy, she made a pilgrimage to Mont St. Michel, where she found the Benedictine monks of the congregation of St. Maur, established since 1624. Then she took the road to Rambervillers, making a stop at St. Maur des Fossés.

The stay at Rambervillers, which seemingly should have been a rebirth, was in fact rather short. In 1650, they found themselves in the midst of war again between the Spanish and French. The town was taken and taken back, always with the attendant pillaging. "The talk is only about swords, fire, and famine," the Prioress wrote to Jean de Bernières. "The few people who remain in the area are almost in despair, such are the many extreme evils here... Our poor house is always full of people who rush here to avoid the first furious blows that the soldiers discharge on those they meet."

In the midst of this storm, she was overwhelmed with interior sufferings. It was proposed to her that she leave the town and become an abbess in France. Instead, she dreamed of making herself forgotten in some unknown monastery, in order to live there "in ennothingment." Bernières judged that these desires for ennothingment came from God, but he did not think that the Mother could abandon her daughters. He wrote:

> I would not abandon the poor house of Rambervillers, even if you are forced to leave this town.... It is much better for you to withdraw to Paris, to get some living there and find your refuge there ... than to have a convent where you can live as a solitary or become an abbess.

> Divine Providence having fixed you where you are, you
> must die there of obedience and of death on the Cross.

The gentleman from Caen had the last word. But Mectilde could not dream of transporting the entire community to Paris. She sent some nuns to Germany, others to Burgundy, left six at Rambervillers, and on March 1, 1651, left for Paris with four young sisters, resolved to find, in the great city, the means to secure a living for her dispersed flock, waiting till she was able to regroup them under her leadership. It was in Paris that God had in store for her the great work for which He had prepared her for such a long time.

Having left the inferno of Rambervillers in search of a little calm, Mother Mectilde found Paris in fire and blood. The Fronde of the Princes had started a civil war there, bringing in its wake the most dreadful misery. First, she had some trouble locating the little group from St. Maur, who were taking refuge in a wretched lodging in Faubourg St. Germain. They were provisionally set up in a building in the Rue du Bac, called *Bon Ami*. It was complete destitution: no linens, no beds, and the necessity of living entirely on alms. To make matters worse, Mother Mectilde fell gravely ill, and they thought it necessary that she receive the last Sacraments. In these sorrowful hours, she showed herself to be completely resigned. As soon as she had convalesced, she wrote to Bernières:

> God has placed me in death and led me back to life. Is it
> not right that I adore Him in all the uncertainties of life and
> death? My soul always remained in Him, and in whatever
> fashion He has dealt with me, my whole soul continually
> remained in a complete surrender to His holy will, without
> any other intention than to be—whether well or ill, living
> or dead—the victim of His love.

From time to time the "little Sisters from Lorraine," as they were called, received the visit of one of the great ladies who desired to solace such miseries. On the last Sunday of August 1651, a carriage stopped before the door of the *Bon Ami*. Two ladies descended: one of them was Vialart de Herse, widow of the president of Parliament and mother of the holy bishop of Chalons, who had been coming for some time to help the sisters; the other was politely distant, unknown to them. She was the Countess of Châteauvieux, who accompanied her friend, but without any particular intention of interesting herself in the poor community. She showed herself vaguely gracious and left an offering, and the two ladies took their leave. Why, then, during the days that followed, could she not take her thoughts off that face of the Prioress, both gracious and grave? That is God's secret. In truth, that visit, apparently indifferent and fortuitous, marked a date of importance in the work being prepared.

She was born Marie de la Guesle. In 1628, she had married René de Vienne, Knight, Count of Châteauvieux and Confolens. They had had only one daughter, Françoise, married since November 15, 1649, to Charles, Duke of Vienville. Madam de Châteauvieux did not have a special attraction to cloisters; she more willingly visited hospitals, to which she gave with great generosity. She was deeply religious, had a lively and curious mind, was agreeably talkative (as one knew how to be in those times) and liked talking. One day, she returned to the Rue du Bac with some friends; they formed a circle around Mother Mectilde, and the Countess turned the conversation to prayer, in which, she declared, she experienced great difficulties. Mother Mectilde gave her advice in a few words, but with much clarity and warmth, for she also had the gift of conversation. Madam de Châteauvieux was conquered. "Ah! My good Mother, what I have been looking for such a long time, what I have not found in any book, you come and tell me in a few words. No one has ever told me so much, and I am content!"

A few days later, with the authorization of her director, Fr. de Bréda, priest of St. André des Arts, the Countess begged her holy friend to become her director. After keeping a great reserve for many days, Mectilde wrote to her new spiritual daughter:

> I have only one reason for being reluctant to agree to what you ask of me: it is the depth of the impurity that is in me, which is truly capable of destroying the holiness that God desires to place in your heart. . . . If you wish to ask Our Lord truly to ennothing me, then I give myself to Him for what He desires me to be for you . . . I am indeed more concerned with your interests than my own and it seems to me that my soul has been entrusted with your soul in a very particular manner. . . . I will offer myself in Holy Communion tomorrow for your welfare. . . . If God desires that I be your "godmother," He desires that you be my daughter in Jesus Christ. It is in Him that I have conceived you; I swear before heaven that I desire you and welcome you only for Him.

However, despite the generosity of the Countess and some of her friends, the situation of the little group of nuns remained very wretched. From various sides, Mother Mectilde continued to be urged to accept the position of abbess or prioress. The Countess learned with displeasure of these propositions that risked separating her from the one who was doing her so much good. It was she who, one day, ventured to suggest another resolution to her. "You cannot dream," she said to Mother Mectilde, "of going back to Rambervillers, in view of the continuing hostilities. Why should your community not have a regular house in Paris?" Bernières was consulted; he was of the same mind as the Countess. He wrote to Mectilde: "There you will have a little peace and you will end the constant travels you are obliged to make."

Overcome with joy, Madam de Châteauvieux immediately busied herself with mobilizing her friends to provide help. She was successful with three especially: the Marquess of Boves, cousin of Madam de Mouy; Madam de Cessac, cousin of Madam de Montgomery, and daughter of the much-missed Mr. de Torp; and Madam de Mangot, widow of a Master of Petitions. The Countess had "an active and very resourceful mind and a prompt and sure judgment, an energetic and opinionated character."[18] She was the soul of the project. This "energetic and opinionated" character served Mother Mectilde in every way, because though her friend accepted the idea of a house, she did not agree in the least to the idea of being superior of it. The Countess appealed to all arguments, brought in teachers and confessors, and finally called on a bishop, who won the day. "I was then," said a smiling Mother Mectilde,

> very often arguing with Our Lord. He wanted me to do something, but I did not want to. My whole desire was to keep myself hidden. I wished to be deaf, blind, mute, so that, unable to do anything, I could apply myself uniquely to God alone. But in the end, He did not want that, and He overturned all my plans.[19]

Finally, the contract was completed and signed on August 14, 1652, by the four foundresses. This contract is of great interest because it places in relief a thought which little by little came to light in the soul of Mother Mectilde and in those of the foundresses.

From her childhood, Mother Mectilde had always felt a very ardent love for the Eucharist. The solitaries of Caen were affiliated with the famous *Company of the Holy Sacrament of the Altar*, of which the local group had for its head Bernières himself, since the death of the Baron of Renty in 1649.[20] In their connections

---

[18] Dourlens, *Vie de la Très Révérende Mère Mechtilde*, 176.

[19] Ibid., 179.

[20] Cf. M. Souriau, *Le mysticisme en Normandie au XVIIe siècle* (Paris: Perrin, 1923), 41 ff.

with Mother Mectilde, Bernières and Fr. Chrysostom had insisted on daily Communion. The former had even had to dispel certain scruples of his "dearest daughter." She wrote to him on August 28, 1645:

> I must speak to you about our Communions. In the past, you ordered me to receive Communion daily. I will tell you that I was tempted many times not to persevere in this, seeing my horrible unworthiness and that my soul is totally impure. The fear took hold of me and then the thought of your command strengthened me and made me go to Communion.

The 17th century was a Eucharistic century. It had this character in reaction to the Calvinists, who denied the Real Presence; it was so also in the thought of reparation—reparation for the sacrileges committed by the soldiery during the wars which for too long laid waste the kingdom, and for those committed by magicians and sorcerers, at that time very numerous. This aspect of reparation had affected Marie de Vallées, who, through St. John Eudes, was connected to the Hermitage. The intention of adoration and reparation had inspired, in a great number of rural parishes as well as urban ones, the foundation of confraternities of the Holy Sacrament, often very active, like the one that Simon de la Vigne, priest of St. Peter's in Caen (one of the regulars at the Hermitage) had established in his parish, which lacked "only the practice of perpetual adoration to be perfect," it was said.[21] The practice of Benediction spread, in spite of certain oppositions. Here and there appeared groups specially dedicated to adoration of the Host, of which the most well known was the nuns of Port Royal, established in Paris in 1633 under the direc-

---

[21] *Manuel de dévotion envers Notre Seigneur Jésus Christ au Très Saint-Sacrement de l'Autel* (Caen: Poisson, 1704). This manual was dedicated to M. de La Vigne, who was one of the close friends of St. John Eudes.

tion of Sebastian Zamet, bishop of Langres, and of the famous Mother Angélique.

The spiritual atmosphere of the times was therefore permeated with Eucharistic fervor. Mother Mectilde herself was imbued with it and it was little by little, under this influence, that she was led to the conviction that her vocation was to given an efficacious and permanent form to these tendencies.

One day she found herself at the home of the Marquess of Boves, waiting, in a little *salon,* to be led into the larger one. She was deeply struck by the sight of a painting representing the punishment of some vestal virgins unfaithful to their vocation. A connection was suddenly made in her mind between the role of the vestal virgin maintaining the sacred flame and what could be the role of an institute of virgins before the Host, guarding, without interruption, the sacred flame of adoration and love. This idea haunted her, and in another visit, she opened her mind to Madam de Boves:

> Madam, the idolaters will one day be our condemnation and that of Christians, who, in their churches, have so little respect for the Most Holy Sacrament. What! Should we not do for God what the pagans did for their false gods.... Why should the virgins on earth not sing perpetually the song of the angels before His altars?

All her memories of horrors previously seen during the war, all her reflections on the love of Jesus in the Eucharist and on the indifference of Christians, all that she knew of the blasphemous use made, in certain places, of the sacred species, the denials and sarcasm of heretics—all this crystallized around the idea that arose, all of a sudden, in the little *salon* of Madam de Boves. And on August 14, 1652, one can read, in the contract signed by Madam de Châteauvieux and her three friends, that a sum of thirty-one thousand pounds, which they undertook to pay, must ensure the foundation of a monastery of nuns from the reformed order of St. Benedict, so that, continually day and night, the Most Holy and Most August Sacrament of the Altar might be adored by the souls consecrated to God in the said monastery, in order to repair, as much as possible, the failures of devotion, the contempt, profanations, sacrileges and dishonors rendered, perpetrated, and presently committed against this Most Adorable Sacrament, in the course of the misfortunes caused by the war which at present afflicts the whole of France, and in order to obtain from God a lasting peace through the whole kingdom, and for the preservation of the king; also to make up for the lack of devotion, inability, and ignorance or malice of all persons who do not adore the Most Holy Sacrament of the Altar and for the multitude of others who will never adore It.

The act of foundation gave to Mother Mectilde a period of two years for the execution of the project. The first obstacle was to obtain the authorization of the Abbot of St. Germain des Prés, who was in charge of the area in which the Sisters then resided. This abbot was none other than the Duke of Verneuil, Henry of Bourbon, one of the illegitimate sons of Henry IV. He was a high and powerful person, loaded with ecclesiastical benefices, but not really a man of the Church. The prelate flatly refused, not on his own account, but because the Queen, Anne of Austria, alarmed at the number of communities set up in that quarter of the town—of which many lived on alms, while others, for lack of funds, had had to be dispersed—had explicitly asked that no more be allowed. An effort made through someone close to the Queen, the Duke of Vieuville, superintendent of finances, father of the son-in-law of Madam de Châteauvieux, had no success. Meanwhile, it was a vow made by a holy priest, Fr. Picoté, friend of Fr. Olier, in the name of and at the request of the Queen during the most tragic days of the Fronde, a vow which was found to coincide with the project of Mother Mectilde, that produced success. Anne of Austria, to whom Fr. Picoté had spoken of the latter, wrote to the Duke of Verneuil, who happened to be her illegitimate brother-in-law:

> My brother, there was a time when I made a vow to use every means that would be most proper in order to give honor to the Most Holy Sacrament of the Altar, in reparation for the sacrileges committed during these unfortunate wars, and, as we have found this cannot be better done than by the establishment of a house of nuns whose the principal concern would be praise and unceasing adoration, and to pray day and night for the peace of the kingdom and for the preservation of the king, I have cast eyes on Mectilde of the Blessed Sacrament, prioress of Rambervillers, who is a person of great merit and distinguished piety. I desire that you give the permissions necessary for this establishment and that you supply whatever depends on you in order to make this succeed for the discharge of my conscience and for the public edification.

Bernières was kept informed of all these proceedings, and thus of the anxieties of his "very dear sister" in the face of the responsibilities which manifested themselves. He settled the matter neatly: "Since all these holy souls advise you to do what is in question, you ought to follow their opinion."

The goodwill of the Queen and of the Abbot of St. Germain des Prés were henceforth secured. The prelate thought it good to entrust the care of the particulars of the business to his vicar general, Dom Placid Roussel, prior of the Abbey. Dom Roussel—he scarcely deserved his name of Placid—was surely a holy man but he was not the most agreeable. Harsh in manners and speech, punctilious and stubborn, he had a talent for finding difficulties where no one else saw them. Many times Mother Mectilde and the Countess were tempted to abandon everything.

"We went to see the Reverend Father Prior who upsets every-thing as much as possible." Thus Mother Mectilde expressed her-self in a letter to a friend. She declared herself "annihilated" from his constant refusals, but did not lose confidence. Madam de Châteauvieux, equally upset but less tolerant, fell seriously ill.

Mother Mectilde prayed, humbled herself, did penance, was consoled by extraordinary spiritual favors; and one day when she was at the bedside of her friend, whose condition continued to be troubling, the unexpected authorization was brought to her from the terrible Dom Roussel, with the authority to proceed—from the following day even—with the exposition of the Holy Eucharist.

The next day was March 25, 1653. The solemn Mass was chanted in the poor chapel, which was attended by a large num-ber of the faithful, notified at the last moment. During this Mass, Mother Mectilde had a vision: the Virgin Mary, bearing the emblems of an abbess, who presented to Jesus the Host the hum-ble community and the work that she had begun. "My dearest daughter," Mother Mectilde wrote to the Countess,

> I greet you in the transports of my joy; it could not be deeper. All that paradise loves and adores . . . I possess, thanks to you. Who would not be carried away with admi-ration at the sight of God's goodness, who allows me to bear, with a real status, the title of Victim of the Most Holy Sacrament!

"The title of Victim." We should take note of these words. The work of Mother Mectilde will not be only the work of adoration. The nun of the Blessed Sacrament is offered like a victim to the One who was on the Cross, who is in the Mass, and who remains, in the Host, the victim of sinners and sacrileges.

Meanwhile, when she was able to go about, Madam de Châ-teauvieux asked for an audience with the Queen Mother. The question was to obtain letters patent from the King authorizing the foundation of the Institute. Despite some opposition, these were signed in May 1653. At Rambervillers, the community had not, by design, re-elected Mectilde as prioress, who had finished the three years' term, so that she could have her hands completely free for the foundation.

They could not remain in the Rue du Bac, which they found too small. The Countess of Rochefort, a friend of Mother Mectilde, leased to her a much more spacious house, which she owned in Ferou Street. The house was quickly prepared, and on March 12, 1654, Dom Roussel installed the sisters there and established them in the cloister. This was an unforgettable solemnity. The Queen came to it, spontaneously, with a numerous cortege, amidst the acclamations of the people. The dignified ease and nobility with which Mother Mectilde received her Sovereign were noted. The Queen had asked the *Musique du Roi* to take part in the ceremony. This was a moving moment, in which Anne of Austria was seen to come forward, near the column surmounted by a lighted candle, put the rope around her neck, and kneeling, pronounce in a clear voice, amid the tears of those present, the words of the Act of Reparation:

> My God and my Savior, Jesus Christ, true God and true Man, worthy victim of the Most High, living bread and source of eternal life, I adore you with all my heart in Your divine Sacrament, with the intention of repairing all the irreverence, profanations, and sacrileges committed against You in this aweful mystery. . . .[22]

The next day, in chapter, Mother Mectilde had the Virgin Mary elected as Superior and perpetual Abbess of the house.

It was some months after the installation at Ferou Street that Fr. Eudes came to visit the Sisters. A letter to Bernières on August 21, 1654 tells us about this visit: "We have had the honor of seeing Reverend Fr. Eudes. He has promised me that he will be our advocate with the good Marie." This good Marie was

---

[22] The prayer is translated in full above, 109–11.

Marie des Vallées, with whom Mother Mectilde had the occasion to correspond several times.[23] The latter wrote to her "dear brother" on September 15, "I welcomed the consolation of your letter through which you had the goodness to send word to me regarding what Rev. Eudes told you for us." Unfortunately, we have only allusions to the object of these connections with the Saint.

The establishment at Madam de Rochefort's could only be provisional. A definitive lodging was necessary. A large plot was found and bought in Cassette Street. The first stone or rather the first three stones were placed on the feast of the Ascension 1658, one by the Count of Châteauvieux, who was more and more interested in the work dear to his wife, the second by the Countess, and the third by the young René-François de Vieuville, their grandson, then six years old. This trio, the Count said jokingly, represented the Holy Family. On the feast of the Annunciation in 1659, the Church was blessed by Monsignor Maupas de Tour, bishop of Puy. The community had been installed since the 21st, the feast of St. Benedict.

Everything was not merely joy during these years, so laden with hopes. In December 1652, the faithful Marquess of Boves died. In 1659, it was the "dear and beloved brother," the confidant of every moment and the prudent director, Jean de Bernières. In 1660, another benefactress, Madam Mangot, was lost. Deprived of these precious supports, the foundress was sometimes seized with anxieties in thinking about her responsibilities as Superior. It required nothing less than the unanimous counsel of St. Vincent de Paul, Fr. Olier, Mr. Boudon, and Fr. Hayneuve to reassure her. At this same period, some slanders were spread about, to which she did not respond except by a more complete confidence in God. To crown all, the Cordelier

---

[23] There are three letters of Mectilde to Marie des Vallées in the manuscript of Bayeux.

Fathers, desiring to acquire for themselves an Institute that had begun to attract the attention of fervent souls, contested the legitimacy of the transfer of the foundress from the Order of the Annunciation, which was dependent on them, to the Order of St. Benedict. They contested even the validity of the professions she had received. She had to appeal to Rome, to the Congregation of Religious, and obtain from the Sovereign Pontiff a brief approving her conduct; letters patent from the king, dated June 26, 1662, authorized their publication.

We recall the impression produced on Mectilde by the Rule of St. Benedict, when she came to know it at Rambervillers in 1639. From the time that she had embraced it, she had had only one preoccupation: to observe it and to make it observed with the greatest fidelity possible, as was done in the best reformed monasteries. Perpetual adoration changed none of her dispositions in this regard. She did not see any opposition between her practices and monastic observance. Adoration was for her a humble and splendid flower opening on the Benedictine stem and nourished by its sap. This is what she repeated to her daughters in her conferences in chapter.[24] "Do not be surprised," she told them, "by the election that God made of the children of this great Patriarch" for the work of perpetual adoration and reparation.

> It is a secret that was shown to me in the death of our great Patriarch, who, wishing to bear witness to the love he had

---

[24] The conference we are citing is drawn from a manuscript of collected conferences of Mother Mectilde that we found 20 years ago in an antique bookshop in Caen. The manuscript (end of the 17th or beginning of the 18th century) begins with two letters addressed by Mectilde to the Benedictines of Toul, which seems to indicate the provenance. This conference is from July 11, 1662.

for the Most Holy Sacrament of the Altar, could not show his faith and love in a greater way than to die standing in Its holy presence and give the last beats of his heart to this adorable Host, enclosed in the sacred ciborium, in order to produce, in time, children of his Order who would give to It, till the end of the world, adoration, reverence, the duties of love, and continual reparation. . . .

The Benedictine nun, she continued,

by the faithful practice of the Holy Rule . . . would become completely like a Host and she would enter into a marvelous affinity with Jesus in the adorable Eucharist. We are indebted to our holy Patriarch for this grace, who merited it for us at the moment of his death when he buried the last moments of his life in the divine Eucharist.

Do you see, my sisters, that St. Benedict died standing up to show us that he breathed forth, with the last effort of love, the holy institute that we profess? He conceived it in the Eucharist, to be produced more than twelve centuries later. . . . No, no, my sisters, this was not at all the plan of a human mind; there is no creature who ordered, instituted, or chose it. It is Jesus in the Host who received it from the heart of our great Patriarch Saint Benedict, and I can say, my sisters, that it was taken from no other place than the tabernacle, where this great saint left it in the last instant of his life.

This outlook, at that epoch, was encouraged by Dom Ignatius Philibert, who was Prior of St. Germain from June 9, 1660. As opposed to Dom Placid, he always presented a friendly countenance. Moreover, he was very attached to the observance of the Rule. The first time he made the regular visitation to the monastery of Cassette Street,

it was a delight for him to see the good order that reigned in the whole house, as much for the interior of the nuns, their regularity, their union, their love of penance and quiet, as for their exterior practices, the diligence for adoration, the beauty of the psalmody and chant, the propriety of the adornments, the exactitude of the ceremonies.

He took a keen interest in the house and held the prioress in an esteem and veneration that only grew as he got to know her better. Like her, he was persuaded that the Institute was destined to expand and that, consequently, precise statutes were necessary. At the advice of Dom Audebert, superior general of the Congregation of St. Maur, and Dom Brachet, his assistant, he worked on these in concert with Mother Mectilde. It was thus that *The Constitutions for the Administration of the Benedictine Nuns of the Most Holy Sacrament and the Declarations on the Rule of St. Benedict Explaining Their Spirit*, were able to appear. Dom Philibert put a year into establishing them, with the help of notes from Mother Mectilde. "It is," says Martène, "a work as judicious as it is full of piety, and testifies at once to his understanding of the holy Rule and to his talent for the guidance of souls."[25]

From that time on, Mother Mectilde's life was divided between the direction of her daughters and the foundation of monasteries, which, as she had foreseen, increased the beneficent influence of her work. We cannot here follow Mother Mectilde in her foundations, which ought to have their own special study. Let us be content with indicating them. The first was in Toul in 1664. In 1665, she received the aggregation of Rambervillers, and in 1669, that of Our Lady of Consolation in Nancy. In 1675, she founded the monastery at Monsieur Street in Paris, and in 1677, the one in Rouen. *Bon Secours* in Caen obtained its aggregation in 1685. The year 1688 saw the foundations in Warsaw and Chatillon-sur-Loing. The last foundation was Dreux in 1696. Everywhere, the Foundress met with obstacles, but she was never shaken: "It is by suffering and sorrow," she wrote, "that

---

[25] Cited by D. Ursmer Berlière, *Nouveau supplément à l'Histoire littéraire de la Congrégation de Saint-Maur* (Paris: A. Picard, n.d.), 2:147.

monasteries of the Institute are made; the joy of adoring the Most Holy Sacrament in them will compensate us abundantly for all our troubles."

Obviously, the foundations constituted an important part of the activity of Mother Mectilde. It was a providential expansion of the work to which she had dedicated her life. But where we like to see her is in her daily life, in the midst of her daughters, in the monastery in Cassette Street. That she was much loved by her community, and by the communities she founded, there is no doubt. She had the human qualities that attract: an appearance both noble and gracious, manners full of distinction and urbanity, an easy and pleasant way of speaking, a natural goodwill, and better still, a tenderness and a generosity that were instinctive, fidelity in affections with nobility of character. But all of this was entirely penetrated and imbued with a profound and radiant interior life and by an intense desire to communicate the love of God that was in her. In the world, such a harmony of qualities would certainly have set her in relief. In the cloister, though without cross or crosier, she can certainly take a place in that series of great reforming abbesses who had such an important role in the "great century." She was profoundly humble, however, completely penetrated, as she said, with her nothingness and her abjection. That was her path for attaining divine love, precisely the one indicated by St. Benedict. But there was nothing affected about her. She never posed when it came to holiness, although the attainment of sanctity to please Jesus was the first of her cares. Perpetual adoration, which seemed a novelty at the time, met with approval among the wide Christian public, which explains the triumphs that often welcomed Mother Mectilde in her travels.

It is certain that in the religious society of the time, and we can say it was all of society, Mother Mectilde had an enormous influence, as can be surmised from her immense correspondence— more than 10,000 letters between 1641 and 1698. All these deeply spiritual people were often great letter writers, among whom one finds all the notable personalities of the religious world: Anne of Austria, the dowager Duchess of Orléans, the Queen Maria-Theresia, St. John Eudes, Bernières-Louvigny, Fr. Chrysostom, Henri Boudon, Dom Louis Quinet, the Abbot of Etival, the Abbot of Roquelay, Marie des Vallées, and a number of the great names of France. Many, above all among these latter, asked for advice and even spiritual direction. The letters that she exchanged with Jean de Bernières are in particular of special importance for truly understanding the interior life of these two "solitaries" and the currents of Norman mystical spirituality.

With her dear daughters and with her friends, Mother Mectilde was preoccupied above all with the glory of God and the salvation of souls. It was to secure both of these that she led them in the ways of immolation and reparation. But she knew how to sympathize with human suffering. She did not overwhelm; she knew how to support and console with tact and delicacy: "My heart is completely full of zeal, tenderness, and love for all that affects you," she wrote to the Duchess of Orléans, "but much more for heavenly things than for earthly things, although I do not forget them in my poor, unworthy prayers." It deserves notice how, without giving offense in anything but with a gentle tenacity, little by little she brought the Duchess first to a quarter of an hour of prayer, then to frequent Communion. Her monastic gravity was tempered with a smile. She had wit and of the best kind, which she kept mild. There is, in all her correspondence, as there was in her conversation, something gracious, spontaneous, and charming.

We recall the harsh lessons of Fr. Chrysostom. Benedictine discretion quickly tempered what was too severe in them. Mother Mectilde made austerity consist, above all, in fidelity to observance and obedience through love. But she did not want health to be compromised. "My poor children, I do not want them to suffer. Let us do whatever is possible that they may be in good health." "Take care of your health. Get some rest. . . ."

From this point of view, she is closer to Dom Louis Quinet than to Fr. Chrysostom.

Precision in the Constitutions and the Observances was always a priority for her. She worked on these, as we noted, with Dom Philibert. In the *Rules for the Offices* which she redacted in 1688, she manifests the spirit which animates this concern: "The Holy Spirit," she wrote, "has put a grace and benediction in each observance and work of holy religion, and one executes it worthily if one sees in it the will of God and remembers the title of Victim of Jesus in the Most Holy Sacrament." The observances were, moreover, only ways of applying the Rule. We have already mentioned the esteem Mother Mectilde had for these. She kept this constantly in view in her redaction of the Constitutions of the Institute. When Dom Claude Martin, one of the most famous spiritual authors of the Congregation of St. Maur, published his *Practice of the Rule of St. Benedict,* which was to have considerable success, she asked the Superior General, Dom Benoît Brachet, for the authorization to issue a text adapted to the Eucharistic vocation of her daughters. She published it in 1687 under the title of *Spiritual Exercises or the Practice of the Rule of St. Benedict for the Use of the Benedictine Nuns of the Blessed Sacrament*.

She had an eminently liturgical piety. The letters of direction she wrote to the Duchess of Orléans, in which she leads the Princess unceasingly to the mysteries celebrated by the Church, form a genuine collection of liturgical meditations. While Dom Philibert dedicated his last forces to editing the text of the *Constitutions*, Mother Mectilde prepared a *Ceremonial*, of which the first part appeared by itself in 1668, and she worked on the *Propers of the Feasts and Offices of the Congregations of Benedictine Nuns of Perpetual Adoration of the Blessed Sacrament*, which she had approved by the Cardinal of Vendôme, at the time of His journey to Paris. She had the taste of her century for the splendor of churches, the richness of altars, of tabernacles, of sacred vessels—in short, for what Huysmans has called "luxury for God."

She liked the pomp of ceremonies, the beauty of chant, and the exact performance of rites. On great occasions, she willingly accepted the *Musique du Roi* and she kept up good relations with Nivers, court organist, and with his wife.

But what she had at heart above all was the spirit of the Institute. It is a matter to which she constantly returns in her letters and conferences, which her nuns transcribed and of which copies were shared with the public. Several small works were drawn, later on, from these conferences.

When the Abbot of Etival, the most reverend Epiphane Louys, had become one of the supporters of the Institute, she asked him for a series of works intended to establish the spirituality proper to her Benedictines. This was the origin of the *Mystical Conferences*, the *Meditations on the Feasts Proper to the Institute*, and above all, two volumes: *Nature Immolated by Grace, or The Practice of Mystical Death for the Instruction of the Benedictine Religious Consecrated to Perpetual Adoration of the Blessed Sacrament*, which appeared in 1674, and *The Immolated and Ennothinged Life of Novices Who Intend to Offer Themselves as Victims to the Son of God in the Congregation of Benedictine Nuns of Perpetual Adoration of the Blessed Sacrament*. This latter was published in the same year as a follow-up to the preceding work.

In the first of these books, Fr. Epiphane establishes with great precision that the religious of the Blessed Sacrament are the Adorers of the Son of God in the Eucharist, that they are Reparators in imitation of Jesus Christ, and that they are Victims, the victims of Jesus, who are entirely given over to Him in this capacity, following the example of Jesus Himself, completely given over to His Father to satisfy His justice, as the victims of ancient times could not do. Mother Mectilde never ceased to tend to this ideal of Adorer, Reparator, and Victim, in self-forgetfulness and self-offering. From the first day of her connection with the group of mystics from Caen, we see her aspiring to "ennothingment" for God. She was this way until the end. "Oh!

What a martyrdom life is," she exclaimed in one of her last letters to Bernières. "All created things increase the sufferings of the soul that longs for heaven." She had it, this love, this *cupio dissolvi et esse cum Christo*,[26] but she longed less to die than to do the will of the Beloved—whether it was life or death. She was His victim. That was her way. She came thus to love suffering and then was no longer able to do without it. In 1670, she wrote:

> Oh! Truly happy is the soul who seeks only to please her Savior, in delivering herself to suffering as the prey of His justice, as the victim of His love. . . . I tremble when I see a soul who does not suffer, it seems to me that she is as if buried in nature. . . . The Finding of the Holy Cross is a feast that happens every day, since every day we find suffering, but it is not the same with its Exaltation.[27] Nothing is rarer than to see trials honored and accepted. . . . What the soul loses when she is found without those humiliations that are the most precious pledges of divine love! . . . But in order to discover the grace that is hidden in them, we must consider them from the point of view of God and receive them from His divine hand. Our Lord, stretched out on the Cross, looked more at the will of His Father than at the executioners who crucified Him. . . .

Handed over, like Jesus, to the Father's good pleasure, she found her consolation before the Host or near the Cross, and in the wounds of Jesus.

---

[26] Cf. Phil 1:23: *Desiderium habens dissolvi, et esse cum Christo.* Having a desire to be dissolved and to be with Christ.

[27] In the Western liturgical tradition, there were two feasts of the Cross: September 14 in the Roman tradition was (and remains) the feast of the exaltation of the Holy Cross, while the Gallican tradition observed a feast of the Cross on May 3. When these two traditions combined, May 3 was kept as the *finding* of the Holy Cross, referring to its discovery in Jerusalem by the Empress Helena around the year 327, while September 14 commemorated the rescue of the true Cross from the Sassanid Persians in the year 629.

In this ardent search for love, she never let go of the hand of Mary, knowing that without her she could not take a step toward Jesus. She had entrusted to Mary all her communities, for which she desired that Mary be the sole Abbess. She had given her soul and the souls of all her daughters to Mary, judging that these victims would be pleasing only if presented by Mary.

Like all those whose life is long, Mectilde knew the melancholy of separations, despite new friendships. She saw depart, each in turn, those souls who had been attached to hers for the accomplishment of her mission, and who in various capacities had entered her life. One by one they disappeared: Anne of Austria; Dom Quinet; the beloved sister remaining in the world and her husband, Colonel l'Huillier, always so dedicated; the Duchess of Orléans; Dom Philibert... Also the old friend, who had been the helper in all her works, the confidante, the spiritual daughter, the one whom Mectilde affectionately called "my Countess," Madam de Châteauvieux. In order to be even more closely joined, Mother Mectilde had given her the habit of the Order.

The holy Prioress was surrounded by affection as much in her Monastery and Institute as in the world. She thanked God for it. She thanked God for the work for which she had been the instrument, truly obliged, despite her profound humility, to recognize that her life of suffering and love had been fruitful. "I feel drawn and urged to go to God," she said. "Only sorrow from my poor daughters stops me, but they must prepare themselves for it and soon." Her last illness was long and painful, but full of consolation and peace. She slipped away gently on April 6, 1698, Quasimodo Sunday, about two in the afternoon, at the age of 83 years, 3 months, and 6 days. Her body was buried in the monastery. The destruction during the French Revolution caused the exact location of her tomb to be lost.

Afterword

A School of Benedictine Spirituality from the 17th Century: The Benedictines of Perpetual Adoration

Dom Jean Leclercq, OSB
Abbey of Clervaux

THE WORKS BROUGHT to completion in 1975 for the centenary of the death of Dom Guéranger made it possible to show the Benedictine authenticity and, at the same time, the cultural limits of the monastic restoration of which he was the craftsman at Solesmes, of those in other nations which derived from or were influenced by his, and of all those of the 19th century.[1] Authenticity and limits: these two terms are suitable for all the foundations and restorations which have taken place in the course of an ancient tradition of fifteen centuries. There is a publication underway which invites us to verify this hypothesis regarding one of the institutes of Benedictine life which has existed the longest, without interruptions, even to our own day: it is the documentation on Catherine de Bar, foundress of the Benedictines of Perpetual Adoration in the 17th century, of which a first volume has appeared, with others set to follow.[2] Right from the first volume, it appears clearly that the "authenticity" has a much greater place than the "limits."

[1] *Le renouveau solesmien et le renouveau religieux du XIXe siècle*, in *Studia Monastica* 18 (1976): 157–95.

[2] *Catherine de Bar, 1614–1698. Mère Mectilde du Saint-Sacrement, Fondatrice de l'Institut des Bénédictines de l'Adoration Perpétuelle du Très Saint-Sacrement de*

Diverse Influences and Benedictine Synthesis

It is not necessary here to trace the well-known biography of Catherine de Bar, but rather to discern the traditions in which her work sinks its roots. So it will be sufficient first to recall briefly the principal dates of her life.[3]

Born in Lorraine in 1614, she entered in 1631 and made profession in 1633 in the monastery of the Annunciades at Bruyères, which was then devastated by war and forced to disperse. She was received in 1638 at the Benedictines of Rambervillers, who were in the current of reform of the Vannists, and she made profession the following year. Obliged to emigrate again, from Lorraine she arrived in France; she stayed in the monastery of the Benedictines of Montmartre, established a small monastery close to that of the Benedictine monks of Saint-Maur-des-Fossés, and came in contact with Saint-Germain-des-Prés.

In 1653, she founded her institute, whose houses very soon multiplied in France and especially in Normandy, as well as in Lorraine and in Poland; after her death, which occurred in 1698, it would extend itself into still other countries of Europe. Today it counts forty monasteries.

In the different regions in which she lived, and in the successive stages of her life, she was marked by a number of influences. That which she received from Lorraine has been underlined by a specialist in the history of the province, M. Pierre Marot.[4] An expert on 17th-century spirituality, Louis Cognet, has added his

---

l'Autel. Documents Historiques, 1640–1670 (Rouen: Bénédictines du Saint-Sacrement, 1973), hereafter cited as DH.

[3] See Canon G. A. Simon's biography in the present volume. See DH 324 for a "Chronologie de la vie de Mère Mectilde" and 329–31 for a bibliography; in addition, Y. Chaussy, *Les Bénédictines et la réforme catholique en France au XVIIe siècle* (Paris, 1975), 371–77, has a brief and dense biography. Others have subsequently been published.

[4] DH 7–21.

valuable contribution.[5] Among the Annunciades, where Catherine lived at the beginning, the spirituality was inspired by the mystics of the North and by Benet Canfield: hence there was a great insistence on interiority and on the mystical life.[6] But the monastery of Rambervillers, where she settled, was under the influence of the Congregation of Saint-Vanne, which represented a rigorous reform, fruitful in doctrinal writings of a very traditional character.[7] Its founder, Dom Didier de la Cour, had had as a disciple Dom Antoine de Lescale, who had favored Catherine's entrance into the Benedictines.[8] Likewise, in Lorraine, she was helped by the Premonstratensian Epiphane Louys,[9] who always remained connected to her, sent her spiritual letters, and composed two works of Benedictine spirituality for her and her Institute. No air-tight divisions existed between the different traditions, and the greatest minds knew how to respect and encourage those to which they did not belong. Thus, the celebrated Mère de Blémur, a Benedictine, published a life of Saint Peter Fourier, the reformer of a congregation of Canons Regular of Saint Augustine. And when the nuns from Lorraine settled in Paris, they were protected by Saint Vincent de Paul.[10]

---

[5] Conference given at the Institut Catholique of Paris, February 8, 1958, in DH 23–33.

[6] Ibid., 24–25.

[7] "Spiritualité vanniste et tradition monastique," in *Revue d'ascetique et de mystique* 36 (1960): 214–31.

[8] DH 16, 220, 249.

[9] Dom Epiphane Louys, abbot of the Premonstratensians of Etival (Vosges). Born at Nancy in 1615, he got to know Mother Mectilde at Rambervillers and became her most faithful supporter. A mystic and man of action, author of many works, he wrote several for the Benedictines of the Most Holy Sacrament. Pierre Marot speaks (DH 21) of a collection of letters of spiritual direction from Dom Epiphane to Mother Mectilde, published after his death on 24 September 1682. Cf. Dom Collet, "Vie manuscripte de Mère Mectilde," in the archives of the abbey of Pradines.

[10] DH 20–21.

In Paris, Catherine de Bar lived in an environment which was heir to a Benedictine tradition coming from the Middle Ages, but which did not exclude the riches transmitted by other spiritual currents: the abbess of Montmartre, Marie de Beauvilliers, was in fact "very close with the Capuchins and the Oratorians and, among the Capuchins, in first place naturally with Benet Canfield." For him "the whole life of piety is summed up in union with the will of God. God is essentially the Divine Will…" This tendency was completed—one would be tempted to say "corrected"—by that which came to Catherine during her stay in Normandy from Jean de Bernières, the founder of a house for retreats, called the Hermitage and situated near an Ursuline monastery in which he had a sister. Now, like Father de Condren and Father de Saint-Jure who also exercised an influence on Catherine, Bernières had a spirituality totally centered on Christ. At Saint-Maur-des-Fossés, Catherine's spiritual director was the Capuchin Father Chrysostom de Saint-Lô, who was also director of Bernières. Hence, as Cognet has observed, during this whole period preceding the foundation of her institute, Catherine de Bar received diverse influences which she knew how to "assimilate so as to make of them a personal synthesis."[11]

The Decisive Influence of the Maurists

Nonetheless, it was above all during what one could call her "Maurist period" that the characteristic spirituality of Catherine de Bar, now become Mother Mectilde of the Blessed Sacrament, received its definitive orientation. The idea of founding an institute where perpetual adoration of the Most Holy Sacrament would be practiced had come to her from Lorraine, where, as Calvinism was spreading everywhere, there was a desire to make

[11] DH 26.

up for its refusal to acknowledge the Real Presence. This manner of reacting, with devotion or theology, was not without precedent in monasticism. Long ago a monk of Liège, Alger, before entering at Cluny, had written to refute certain errors whose origin went back to Berengarius of Tours, and which had spread at Liège at the beginning of the 12th century.[12] Thus, in the spiritual circles she frequented, it was suggested to Mother Mectilde to found "a congregation that, keeping the Benedictine observance, would nonetheless introduce adoration of the Most Holy Sacrament—something to which [the observance] lends itself admirably, given the liturgical orientation of its piety."[13] It was at this time that she received valuable help from the monks of the Congregation of St. Maur, and in a special way from those of Saint-Germain-des-Prés. Since these facts have already been established and documented elsewhere,[14] here it will suffice simply to recall them.

The prior of Saint-Germain at the time was Dom Placide Roussel. It was he who in 1656 drew up the document of the formalities for the foundation at Paris. The religious sisters promised to recognize him as "their ordinary superior, to guide them in both temporal and spiritual matters." In 1659, his successor, Dom Bernard Andebert, confirmed that the monastery situated in the Rue Cassette was "under his spiritual jurisdiction." Mother Mectilde did not leave the Rue Cassette. Until her death she remained connected with the religious of Saint-Germain and especially with Dom Ignace Philibert, their superior.

---

[12] L. Brigué, "Alger de Liège," in *Studia eucharistica DCC Anni a condito festo Sanctissimi Corporis Christi* 1246–1946 (Anvers, 1946), 50–60.

[13] DH 28.

[14] "Saint-Germain-des-Prés et les Bénédictines de Paris," in *Revue d'histoire de l'Eglise de France* 43 (1957): 223–30; a special number of this review was also published under the title *Mémorial du XIVᵉ centenaire de l'abbaye de Saint-Germain-des-Prés* (Paris, 1959).

He took in hand the interests of the new monastery of Benedictine nuns during the whole time he remained in Paris, that is,
until his death in 1667. "He established a commission of twelve
members, including Dom Andebert, superior general of the
reformed Congregation of Cîteaux. These were of the opinion
that a congregation to sustain perpetual adoration of the Most
Holy Sacrament was absolutely necessary, and they charged
Mother Mectilde with drafting its statutes." But the *Document
biographique* tells us that the Mother, "not being able to work for
this end, both because of the frequent journeys to which she was
obliged for the foundations of the Institute, and because of the
need to guide her community in the little time that remained,
found herself obliged to ask [Dom Andebert] himself to draft
them, seeing that he had much more competence than she in this
sort of thing, having experience of the Congregation of St.
Maur, within which he had also governed for so long several of
their first houses."

"It was to the Prior of Saint-Germain, in August 1654, that
Mother Mectilde had proposed blessing a great relief image of
the Mother of God, who would be considered the Superior of
the Institute. A little later, on August 24, Mother Mectilde submitted to the Prior the act which she had composed to dedicate
her monastery to Our Lady. By doing this, the Benedictines of
Rue Cassette restored to its vigor an ancient devotion practiced
since the 11th century at Marcilly, under the influence of Cluny.
One can imagine that the erudition of the Maurists was not
unrelated to this restoration of a medieval usage. Dom Bernard
Andebert, monk of Saint-Germain, 'permitted that the aforesaid
offering and its renewal should take place every year on the day
of the Assumption of the holy Virgin. . . .'"[15]

---

[15] DH 238, 98. Cf. "Notre Dame abbesse," in *Priez sans cesse: Trois cents ans
de prière* (Paris, 1953), 175–77, and M. Pigeon, "Sainte Marie abbesse," in
Cîteaux 26 (1973): 68–69.

Not only did the monks of Saint-Germain help the Benedictines of Rue Cassette in the governance of their community, they exercised a direct and decisive influence on the spiritual orientation of the entire congregation of the Benedictines of the Most Holy Sacrament. When needed, they lent their pen and their talents: in 1696, Dom Mabillon composed in the Prioress's name a long and beautiful circular letter on the death of Madame de Blémur. In 1702, a document signed by all the nuns and directed to the Prior of Saint-Germain thanks him for a conference which he gave and asks him to continue helping them. On August 22, 1668, Mother Mectilde besought the Prior of Saint-Germain "to approve and confirm the Bull of erection of their congregation, obtained from Monsignor Vendôme at the time he was legate"; and after the approval of the congregation and its constitutions by Alexander VII, the Benedictines submitted to the Prior of Saint-Germain the formula of profession.

In 1686, Mother Mectilde had the *Spiritual Exercises, or Practice of the Rule of St. Benedict for the Use of the Benedictines of Perpetual Adoration of the Most Holy Sacrament*, printed for her daughters. Now, this is almost nothing other than the work of Dom Claude Martin, entitled *The Practice of the Rule of St. Benedict*. This book, declares Mother Mectilde in a letter published at the beginning of the volume, "can also justly be called 'the Benedictine way of life'; it could suffice for bringing us to the perfection of our state." For this reason, she did not seek a plan different from the one adopted by Dom Claude Martin. She is almost always content with putting the expressions in the feminine; rarely does she modify the wording or propose a different practice. In the chapter on stability, she adapts what was said about stability in the congregation, which was particular to the Maurists, to stability in the enclosure befitting the nuns.

If new chapters were inserted in the service of the proper spirit of the Benedictines of "Perpetual Adoration" and of the practices which derive from this, such as "In what spirit one should make reparation" or "On duties to the holy Virgin as first and perpetual Abbess," these do not destroy in the least the homogeneity of the whole; they merge with the spirituality and teaching which spring from the work. Mother Mectilde is not afraid to affirm that "even if we should lose all the other books, we would always find in this one something to console us," because "it is not lacking in all that is necessary to elevate the soul to the holiness of life to which we must aspire and which our profession requires of us."

Hence, the identity of interpretation of the Rule of St. Benedict among the Maurists and the Benedictines of the Most Holy Sacrament is attested by the Foundress of the latter; for their part, Dom Brachet, who gave permission for the printing, and Dom Claude Bretagne, then Prior of Saint-Germain, who granted the approbation, confirm this agreement.

The monks of Saint-Germain exercised a great influence on these Benedictines who, from Rue Cassette, spread thereafter to different regions of France and numerous nations of Europe. The community of Paris has now been transferred. Until the Revolution, the monks of Saint-Germain helped that house, although in general they were neither chaplains nor confessors. Other monasteries of the Most Holy Sacrament, situated at Rouen, Caen, Châtillon, Dreux, and Bayeux, also benefited from the ministry of the monks of Saint-Germain. As for the houses in Lorraine, that is, at Rambervillers, Toul, and Nancy, they were placed under the spiritual jurisdiction of the Congregation of Saint-Vanne. Currently the Benedictines of the Most Holy Sacrament of Mas-Grenier, in Tarn-et-Garonne, occupy the old monastery of the Maurists. In 1705, two monks of Saint-Germain, Dom Guillaume Laparre and Dom Claude de Vic, busied themselves at Rome to obtain the definitive approval of the Constitutions of the Benedictines of the Most Holy Sacrament. And in our days, in numerous places, they keep alive a spiritual tradition directly inspired by that of the Congregation of Saint Maur.

The Permanent Values of a Spirituality

If we seek now to single out the dominant characteristics of this spirituality, we can reduce them to three.

1. First of all, we find an authentic Christocentrism, in conformity with the purest theological and spiritual tradition. This is explained by the influence of Bérulle, of Condren, of Olier, the great representatives of the "French School" of the time, but above all by the influence of Sacred Scripture and particularly of Saint Paul, the whole being integrated in an interior attitude molded by the liturgy. Certainly, this devotion to Christ is centered on the Eucharist, the mystery about which so many monks, from the 9th to the 12th century, had written;[16] but the Jesus Who is celebrated and adored in It is considered, as in the liturgy, in His Paschal aspect: "You are dead," teaches Mother Mectilde, "and your life is hidden in Jesus Christ"[17]—a traditional theme *par excellence*,[18] as is also its necessary complement: the passage from death "to the new life in Jesus Christ, which is the very grace of Christianity." In fact, Baptism, by incorporating us into Christ, renders us capable of participating in His Priesthood, in His "quality of Priest and Victim." In the Eucharistic Sacrifice, Christ offers Himself and we offer ourselves with Him and in Him. This is the exercise of the royal priesthood of the faithful, brought back to light by Vatican II!

This, it seems to us, is the basis of her doctrine, and it is the same as that of the Church, expressed, in the manner of her time, with remarkable constancy. She takes great care to highlight how this quality of "victim" which she gives to her daughters

[16] Bibliography in "Les méditations eucharistiques d'Arnaud de Bonneval," in *Rech. de théol. anc. et médiév.* 13 (1946): 40–56.

[17] Cited in DH 118; the quotation is Col 3:3.

[18] See, for example, *Pierre le Vénérable* (Saint-Wandrille, 1946), 91–94: "La vie cachée"; G. Penco, "Il monastero sepolcro di Cristo," in *Vita monastica* 17 (1963): 99–109.

"is not a new quality, it is a title which Jesus Christ impressed on you with Baptism." We have seen that it is the priesthood of the faithful. For her, perpetual adoration is not only a homage to the Eucharistic Presence; it should be "a universal renewal of all our life and of all our actions"; she also calls it "continual adoration." It is the putting into practice, the means, and the sign of that Paschal life which is the fruit of the Eucharist—and this, for the extension of the grace of the Sacrifice in us and in the world. She thus unites, in a vital way, adoration and reparation. Because— let us note well—the "reparation" directed to Christ in the Eucharist is always presented by her as a participation in the mystery of the Redemption, in our humble place as redeemed creatures, as members of the Church, which continues this redemptive gestation "until His return." She insists on this in a special way: "There is no one other than Christ Jesus Who can repair His glory and that of His Father." Everything consists in this: "becoming another Jesus Christ."[19]

All asceticism derives from this contemplation of Christ, from this participation in His redemptive contemplation. This teaching is found marvelously developed in a Retreat written in 1662, of which here are some extracts:

> It remains to explain . . . in what this perpetual immolation consists, which the Daughters of the Most Holy Sacrament are bound to make every day, in order to imitate, as much as possible, Jesus Christ immolated unceasingly to His Father.
>
> This perpetual immolation, my sisters, requires two things. First: the pure gaze on God always, as Jesus always gazes on His Father. Second: forgetfulness of ourselves with a wise indifference to an infinity of trifles which make us turn back on ourselves in so many ways: now by affection or desire, and so on; next by fear of some humiliation

---

[19] Cited in DH 118–19.

or anxiety about the privation of some pleasure; now in considering the actions of others, and the thousand similar things which sometimes keep us so occupied and so attached to them that we lose our interior attention to God. And this miserable inclination which turns us toward ourselves has such malignity that it makes us incapable of gazing at God and resembling Jesus in the Host. For we must not separate ourselves from our adorable goal; we should not distance ourselves from our adorable object, since He is our divine model. We must have Him always before our eyes, and do always what He Himself does, since we should follow in His steps.

This is not a chimera or a fantastical position based on unreasonable ideas. No, this is the obligation of the Christian, but it is doubly so for a daughter of the Most Holy Sacrament: to become as much as possible like her Father.

Continue, then, to contemplate what Jesus does in this august Mystery: see how He has nothing else in view but the glory of God, how He forgets His own interests.

Yes, my sisters, this is admirable: Jesus enters into our hearts to celebrate in us an eternal sacrifice, divine, of an infinite merit; this should make us love Holy Communion, because He fulfills in us the office of high Priest and supreme Sacrificer, immolating Himself for the soul who receives Him and rendering a homage of infinite glory to God His Father with His divine sacrifice.[20]

But let us leave this subject, so as to continue showing the two actions which Jesus continually carries out in the Host. The first is a continual gaze at His Father, the second is the salvation of men; and these are the motives of our vocation in our institute: the glory of God and zeal for the conversion of sinners, especially of the profaners of this sacred Mystery. . . .

[20] DH 131.

You are sinners, my sisters, personally and in your brethren. You have sacrificed yourselves to obtain pardon and to repair, if it is possible, the glory stolen from God. You do what Jesus did, although certainly in an infinitely dissimilar manner; you should therefore be resolved to be treated as He. This will never happen to an infinite degree (you would not be capable of it), but according to God's good pleasure and to the degree that will be necessary to satisfy His justice.[21]

This is the exact opposite of a sentimental and individualistic piety. The greatest representatives of the monastic tradition would have recognized themselves in it.

2. Another characteristic of Mother Mectilde's teaching is constituted by her attachment to the life and the Rule of Saint Benedict. From the saint's biography she remembers especially the last of the marvelous facts narrated by Saint Gregory,[22] as she herself declares in a writing entitled *On the Spirit of Saint Benedict*:

If you ask me, my sisters, whence I take what I have said, I dare to assure you that this concerns a secret which it was granted to me to discover in the death of our most holy Patriarch, who, wishing to bear witness to his love for the most holy Sacrament of the Altar, could do so no better than by expiring in its holy Presence. Thus did he render up the last gasps of his heart to that adorable Host, so that his sentiments, enclosed in the sacred ciborium, could in time generate sons of his Order who would, to the end of the world, offer adoration, homage, and continual acts of love and of reparation. [...]

If it were permitted to me to describe in detail the spirit and the dispositions which a Benedictine ought to have, you would see that, practicing faithfully the holy Rule, she

---

[21] DH 132.

[22] *Dialogues* II.37, ed. Morrica (Rome, 1924), 132.

would be similar in everything to a Host, and in Eucharistic adoration would enter into a marvelous relationship with Jesus.

So do you not see, my sisters, that Saint Benedict dies standing up, in order to make us understand that he is causing to blossom, in an exertion of love, the holy institute which we profess? He conceives it in the Eucharist, so that it might be born more than twelve hundred years later![23]

Regarding the Rule of St. Benedict, Mother Mectilde preserves all of its fundamental observances:

The relation and the connection which exists between the Rule of the great Patriarch and the institute of Perpetual Adoration required that this holy Rule should be its basis and foundation; indeed, those who belong to the institute should lead a life austere, penitent, and very separated from the world, in order to be true victims and worthy reparators, and this holy Rule contains all this in an outstanding way. . . .[24]

Her contemporaries, in fact, attest that these religious "follow the Rule of St. Benedict with the most rigorous exactness";[25] "they bring to life again the ancient Rule of St. Benedict and the primitive rigor of its observance, and it pleases God to raise up every so often religious who, aspiring to a holy reform of their Order, may serve as an instrument to bring it about."[26] They merit, therefore, the title of "reformed religious" of this Order.[27]

3. Finally, Mother Mectilde instinctively recovers, because she knows the tradition to which she belongs, many practices which

---

[23] Cited in DH 155–56.

[24] DH 125.

[25] Cited in DH 234.

[26] DH 235.

[27] DH 249.

had been handed on since the Middle Ages. We have already noted this regarding Our Lady as Abbess. The same holds for the devotion to St. John associated with Mary at the foot of the Cross;[28] the clothing *ad succurrendum* which permits people who have lived in the world to "die with the habit of the Order";[29] the very symbolism of this habit, a sign of "life hidden to the world and separated from the world" and a reminder of the Cross of Christ.[30]

Does a Pure "Benedictinism" Exist?

After having reviewed this long history—longer than that of most existing Benedictine congregations—we must pose this question, for two reasons: first, because, as we have seen, the Benedictine tradition was not the only one to exert influence on Mother Mectilde, especially during the period before the foundation of her Institute; and secondly, because, in fact, objections are sometimes raised against their character as "pure Benedictines," on three counts: they go back only to the 17th century; they bear the stamp of the French School; and importance is given to "reparation" in their spirituality. Such remarks require some reflections and suggest some comparisons. These will be taken from the general history of Benedictine life and also from the conditions in which this life has been lived and is still lived today.

---

[28] DH 185. Cf. "Dévotion et théologie mariale dans le monachisme bénédictin," in *Maria. Etudes sur la Sainte Vierge* II (Paris, 1952), 557–58 and 577.

[29] DH 194; cf. "La vêture 'ad succurrendum' d'après le moine Raoul," in *Analecta monastica, Studia Anselmiana* 3 (Rome, 1955), 158–68.

[30] DH 198; cf. *La vie parfaite* (Paris-Turnhout, 1948), 128–29. [At this point, Leclercq dedicates several pages of his study to showcasing then newly-available letters from Mother Mectilde to the Warsaw foundation. These have been omitted here.]

The 17th-Century Tradition and the Others

Any judgment about an institution which has a history presupposes an exact conception of what the tradition is and what it is not. The tradition is not identified with the past, ancient or recent, nor with a bygone period, considered (more or less arbitrarily) as privileged; the tradition is the vital current which runs through and animates the entire development of a spiritual organism, whether personal or collective, from its origins.[31] Hence, it benefits from the contribution of all eras, without being reduced to any of them, while legitimately placing the accent on this or that datum transmitted by them. It therefore entails a choice, or choices, from this inheritance; and since it can never reach a totality, by this very fact it runs the risk of an impoverishment. But it is normal, and even inevitable, that it assumes and makes more or less its own the values proper to the time in which it is lived, and in this there is a source of enrichment.

This type of historical law could be illustrated in the light of many examples. In the English Benedictine Congregation, a 17th-century author, Dom Augustine Baker, has been and is considered as a classic of that institution's spirituality; now, he owes very much to the non-Benedictine writings of the *Devotio moderna*, to Carmelites and Jesuits, and above all to two Capuchins: Benet Canfield (by whom, as we have seen, Mother Mectilde was also inspired) and Constantin de Barbanson.[32] A "monk of the 20th century, a witness of the liturgical renewal," even points out in him this "lacuna": "The liturgy: in this work written for Benedictines, does it occupy perchance the place which we

[31] Cf. "Tradition et ouverture," in *Chances de la spiritualité occidentale* (Paris, 1966), 67–86.

[32] J. Juglar, "Introduction," in Dom Augustin Baker, *La Sainte Sapience ou Les voies de la prière contemplative* (Paris, 1954), xxiii–xxv.

would have expected? One must confess that it does not."[33] But probably the criteria of Benedictinism derived from Solesmes in the 19th century are not at all fitting for the Benedictinism of other times and other lands. In France in the 19th century, Père Muard, not only before his "novitiate à la Trappe" but even afterwards, might make one think that "there is an inescapable closeness between him, founder of La Pierre-qui-Vire, and Saint Francis of Assisi: he himself would not have denied it."[34] And to recognize, for example, that "Dom Guéranger and Père Muard had entirely different monastic conceptions"[35] does not imply any judgment on the greater or lesser Benedictine "purity" of one or the other.

As for Dom Guéranger, it is not necessary to repeat here how much he was imbued with the ideas of his own time, while at times having just and profound intuitions about Benedictine life; with regard to the past, let us merely remember that he was inspired greatly by the Constitutions of the Congregation of Saint Maur,[36] the same ones which had been at the basis of the Constitutions of the Benedictines of Perpetual Adoration. Later, at Sainte-Cécile de Solesmes, an abbess, Cécile Bruyère, sought to introduce into the monastic spirituality of the West certain ideas inspired by Pseudo-Dionysius,[37] which constituted an innovation. And one could go on, citing examples of the same kind furnished by the restorations and foundations which go from the end of the 1800s through all of the 1900s. In short, an institution is no less "purely Benedictine" because it is old than

[33] Ibid., xix.

[34] D. Huerre, *Jean-Baptiste Muard* (La Pierre-qui-Vire, 1950), 352–53; cf. ibid., 313 and 336–37; on Paray-le-Monial, 310.

[35] *Bulletin de l'Abbaye d'Hautecombe* 101 (March 1976): 20.

[36] L. Soltner, *Solesmes et Dom Guéranger (1805–1875)* (Solesmes, 1974), 39.

[37] C. Bruyère, *La vie spirituelle et l'oraison* (Tours, 1950), 416; in the table of citations one finds numerous references to "Denys l'Aréopagite."

another is because it is recent; and the spirituality of the Vannists and the Maurists is as valid as those which had to be established later, after an interruption of historical continuity owing to the revolutionary crisis and the reactions that this provoked.

The Influence of the French School

There is no need to discuss this at length, when, regarding Dom Guéranger, we note with his most recent biographer that "the authors of the French School were always the object of his admiration,"[38] for which it would be in poor taste to criticize him. We merely point out that the French School includes spiritual currents which differ greatly among themselves. In this regard, it is not without interest to observe that Mother Mectilde seems to have realized her synthesis outside of the movement of devotion to the Sacred Heart which, encouraged above all by the Jesuits, developed in many religious milieus.[39] Like all the Catholics of her time, she gave a place in her teaching to the Sacred Heart,[40] but in a manner in conformity with the Benedictine tradition.[41]

Reparation

Reading the texts of Mother Mectilde, we cannot avoid two impressions. First of all, it is clear that reparation is nothing other than a different name for that which has always been called penance and which today we prefer to reconnect with the concept of reconciliation. If we find in her an insistence on the com-

---

[38] Soltner, *Solesmes*, 22.

[39] Her doctrine was formed prior to the revelation at Paray to Saint Margaret Mary Alacoque in 1685; cf. A. Amon, "Cœur (Sacré): au XVIIe siècle," in *Dictionnaire de spiritualité* 2 (1953): 1033–35. Mother Mectilde places herself in the direct line of the tradition.

[40] U. Berlière, *La devotion au Sacré-Cœur dans l'Ordre de St. Benoît* (Paris-Maredsous, 1923), 122–24.

[41] "Le Sacré-Cœur dans la tradition bénédictine au moyen âge," in *Cor Jesu* II (Rome, 1959), 1–28; C. Vagaggini, "La dévotion au Sacré-Cœur chez Sainte Mechtilde et Sainte Gertrude," ibid., 29–48.

pensation to be made for the denials of which the Real Presence was the object, this is of the same order as that which led numerous restorers of monasticism in the 19th century to want to "repair" the impieties of the French Revolution and its consequences as well as the impieties of their contemporaries. On this point, Mother Mectilde participates in the religious culture of the 17th century, as did Père Muard and Dom Guéranger in that of the 19th. All the same, and secondly, the forms of devotion to the Sacred Heart which would enjoy the preferences of the monastic circles of this last era [the 19th century] would be closer to those of the tradition coming from Paray-le-Monial than was the case with Mother Mectilde.

In short, among the Vannists, the Maurists, and the Benedictines of the Most Holy Sacrament, one same authentic sense of liturgical life was expressed, only in a different manner: more marked in the 17th century by simplicity than by solemnity, although the love of the beautiful was not excluded from it. They [the Benedictines of the Most Holy Sacrament] have the same preferences: for simplicity regarding titles, insignia, and dignities of superiors and superioresses, and for the ceremonious forms with which they manifest respect towards them. One cannot say that one of these mentalities is more traditional and more "purely Benedictine" than the other, unless one wishes to reserve these qualifications only for the most ancient inheritance.

This recalling of the past confirms the conclusion to which the general history of monasticism has been leading: the greatest reserve is needed when talking about what is "purely Benedictine"—if "purely" is meant to signify "without any mixture"—and what is not. No institute of this name is "pure" in this sense, and all of those that safeguard the monastic character of the life established by the Rule of St. Benedict are "authentic," regardless of the forms of devotion with which this essential element has been accompanied over the centuries.

*Laudetur Sacrosanctum et
Augustissimum Sacramentum in Aeternum*

CPSIA information can be obtained
at www.ICGtesting.com
Printed in the USA
BVHW030858270720
584433BV00007B/49

9 781621 385219